A Photographic Atlas for Physical Anthropology

Brief Edition

Paul F. Whitehead

Associate Professor,
Department of Science and Mathematics
Capital Community College

and

Curatorial Affiliate,
Division of Vertebrate Zoology
Peabody Museum of National History
Yale University

William K. Sacco

Susan B. Hochgraf

Morton Publishing Company
925 W. Kenyon, Unit 12
Englewood, Colorado 80110
http://www.morton-pub.com

D0139391

BOOK TEAM

Publisher	Douglas N. Morton
Project Manager	Dona Mendoza
Cover & Design	Bob Schram, Bookends
Composition	Ash Street Typecrafters, Inc.

DEDICATION

To my parents, Louise and Victor Whitehead,
and my wife Narinder Kaur Whitehead,
with gratitude for your patience, support and guidance.

Printed in the United States of America

10 9 8 7 6 5 4 3 2 1

ISBN: 0-89582-668-2

Preface

"Alice was beginning to get very tired of sitting by her sister on the bank, and of having nothing to do: once or twice she had peeped into the book her sister was reading, but it had no pictures or conversations in it, 'and what is the use of a book', thought Alice, 'without pictures or conversations?'"

Lewis Carroll—*Alice's Adventures in Wonderland*

The concept of this atlas was formulated as a result of my experience as a student and later as a college faculty member. During my own training, I took courses in human anatomy and histology, and I currently teach these subjects to students who are preparing to become Registered Nurses. They are areas in which many excellent atlases have been available for years. The atlases serve to guide the student and teacher in the laboratory and are essential aids in learning the material outside of the classroom.

My undergraduate major was anthropology with a concentration in physical anthropology at the University of Pennsylvania. I had marvelous professors who thoroughly knew the material and encouraged critical thinking. At the same time, there was no single volume in physical anthropology that served the same role as an anatomy or histology atlas did for those subjects.

This atlas is meant to fill that gap in the literature. It is not meant to be a traditional textbook with drawings and photographs employed primarily to illustrate points made in the text. It is also not meant to be a purely technical work to be used only by professionals and graduate students, although those individuals should find it useful. Rather, it can be used in conjunction with textbooks and original journal article readings to provide a visual representation of the material that physical anthropologists study and discuss. It is both comparative and functional in its approach.

Courses that teach physical anthropology are sometimes more idiosyncratic in their content than are undergraduate courses in some other subjects. In undergraduate human anatomy and physiology for example, the subject is dominated by a few major textbooks and laboratory manuals. Most faculty teach the same basic topics regardless of their particular specialty. Physical anthropology is at the junction between the subdisciplines of anthropology (the study of human culture in a recent or archeological context) and the subdisciplines of biology and geology. Faculty who teach human evolution may

therefore be cultural anthropologists, archeologists, geneticists, comparative morphologists or primatologists (among other fields). The atlas does not specifically cover all of the specialties in physical anthropology, but an effort has been made to cover visually oriented topics that most courses will address.

The major emphasis in the illustrations is on photographs of actual skeletal material, not on idealized representations of morphology. While the latter has heuristic value, and is used at points throughout the atlas, it is important for students to realize that actual material is subject to individual variation. The atlas is unique in its presentation of high-quality, color photographs. Most of these were taken by Mr. William Sacco, a professional photographer with many years of experience with natural history specimens, and the author working together. The photographs are therefore both informative and visually spectacular. We have, on some specimens, retouched cracks, minor breaks, etc. The photographs will be a useful guide for students at colleges and universities that have good collections of osteological material and of fossil casts. The photographs will also be an invaluable visual representation for students who do not have the opportunity to have "hands-on" experience with specimens.

ACKNOWLEDGMENTS

I acknowledge the assistance of many individuals and institutions in the production of this atlas; if anyone is not mentioned, it is an error of omission rather than a lack of gratitude. First, I wish to thank my collaborators in the production of the book, William Sacco and Susan Hochgraf. Their talents and expertise were instrumental in producing a high-quality volume, and it has been a privilege to work with them. I thank their families for tolerating my interruptions of their normal lives with Sunday morning photography sessions, telephone messages, etc. Douglas Morton recognized the need for an atlas in physical anthropology and provided support and genuine interest throughout the project. Thanks to him and all of his staff, especially Christine DeMier and Dona Mendoza. Joanne Saliger, Ash Street Typecrafters, applied her considerable skill and talent to producing a superior product. She shared my vision of producing a unique book and I am grateful.

The production of this atlas would have been considerably more difficult without access to the superb collections of the Divisions of Vertebrate Zoology, Anthropology and Vertebrate Paleontology of the Peabody Museum of Natural History, Yale University. Dr. Richard Burger, Director of the Peabody Museum at the beginning of this project and Professor of Anthropology, supported the concept of the atlas and generously provided access to the human skeletal material from Machu Picchu, Peru. Drs. Andrew Hill and Frank Hole, Curators of Anthropology at the Peabody Museum and Professors of Anthropology, provided permission to use and photograph the skeletal material of both the Division of Anthropology of the Peabody Museum and the Dept. of Anthropology, Yale University. Dr. Jacques Gauthier, Curator of Vertebrate Zoology and Ornithology and Professor of Geology and Geophysics, granted permission to use and photograph material from the Divisions of Vertebrate Zoology and Vertebrate Paleontology. Mr. Tim White, Senior Collections Manager, and Dr. Larry Gall, Systems Office and Executive Editor of Peabody Museum Publications, supported the concept of the atlas and encouraged its completion. The collections managers and staff were uniformly supportive and cheerfully provided access to the specimens: particular thanks to Dr. Roger H. Colten (Collections Manager) and Mr. Gary Aronsen of the Division of Anthropology, Mr. Lyndon Murray (formerly Collections Manager), Mr. Dan Brinkman and Ms. Mary Ann Turner (Registrar) of the Division of Vertebrate Paleontology, and Dr. Kristof Zyskowski (Collections Manager) and Greg Watkins-Colwell of the Division of Vertebrate Zoology and Ornithology.

Dr. Kurt Schwenk, Associate Professor, Dept. of Ecology and Evolutionary Biology, University of Connecticut, Storrs, kindly provided several specimens from the UCONN mammal collection for photography. Skulls Unlimited International allowed me to borrow human skeletal material and consented to publication of the photographs.

Photographs of specimens were graciously provided by a number of colleagues, including: Dr. Brenda Benefit, Dr. Michael Brunet, Mr. Paul Creech, Dr. Eric Delson, Dr. Donald Johanson, Mr. Jon Kalb, Dr. Kenneth A.R. Kennedy, Wolfgang Maier, Ms. Mary Muungu, Dr. Peer H. Moore-Jansen, Ms. Pamela Owens, Dr. Osbjorn Pearson, Dr. David Pilbeam, Dr. Yoel Rak, Dr. G. Philip Rightmire, Dr. Kenneth Rose, Dr. Catherine Skinner, Dr. S. Simone, Dr. Elwyn Simons, Dr. Tom Struhsaker, Dr. Erik Trinkaus and Dr. Xinzhi Wu. The following institutions gave permission for publication of images of their specimens or provided images of the specimens: National Museums of Kenya, Institute of Human Origins and National Museum of Ethiopia, National Museum of Tanzania (Dar es Salaam), Naturmuseum Senckenberg (Frankfurt), Austrian Museum, Laboratoire d'Anthropologie, Universite de Bordeaux (Talence), South African Museum (Cape Town), Institut de Paleontologie Humaine (Paris), Staatliches Museum fur Naturkunde (Stuttgart), Geolosko-Paleontolosko Musej (Zagreb), Rheinisches Landsmuseum (Bonn), Musee de l'Homme (Paris), Museo di Antropologia "G. Sergi" (Dipartimento do Biologia Animale e dell 'Uomo, Universita di Roma "La Sapienza"), Israel Antiquities Authority (Jerusalem), Peabody Museum, Harvard University, Institute of Vertebrate Paleontology and Paleoanthropology, People's Republic of China, Musee Monaco, Texas Memorial Museum of Science and History (University of Texas), Dept. of Palaeontology, Transvaal Museum, and Ministero per i Beni e le Attivita Culturali-Soprintendenza per i Beni Archeologici della Liguria. Particular thanks to: Ato Jara Haile-Mariam, Head of the Authority for Research and Conservation of Cultural Heritage, Ministry of Culture and Information, F.D. Republic of Ethiopia; Ms. Mary Muungu of the Dept. of Palaeontology, National Museums of Kenya; and Professor Xinzhi Wu of the Institute of Vertebrate Paleontology and Paleoanthropology, People's Republic of China.

Cliff Jolly and Bill Sacco reviewed virtually the entire book prior to publication. Eric Delson, Erik Trinkaus and Tom Struhsaker made useful comments on specific sections of the text. John Verano made his notes on the Machu Picchu, Peru specimens available to me before publication of his recent paper, and John Seidel and Aaron Gross gave their professional opinions on dental pathologies for Chapter Seven.

Dr. Ira Rubenzahl, President, and Dr. Mary Ann Affleck, Academic Dean, of Capital Community College have always encouraged my interest in research and publication and I sincerely thank them for their support.

I have had many brilliant and supportive professors, both as an undergraduate and as a graduate student, and it would be impossible to list everyone here. However, my undergraduate experience was a particularly important phase of my life and I wish to specifically thank four anthropologists for their help and the knowledge that they imparted: Dr. Alan E. Mann, Dr. Clifford J. Jolly, Dr. Robert S.O. Harding and Dr. Jacques Bordaz.

Thanks also to the administration and staff of the National Museums of Kenya and the National Museum of Ethiopia, the officials of the Office of the President of Kenya and the Ministry of Culture and Information of Ethiopia, and indeed to my many friends and colleagues in Kenya and Ethiopia who tolerated my American manners and made me feel welcome.

Finally, I wish to thank my family for their patient support. My wife, Narinder, encouraged me in this project. Her cheerfulness and equanimity have balanced the vicissitudes of a major publication effort. My parents, Louise and Victor Whitehead, never told me to follow a specific career, but always asked that I do my best. They probably never understood how a boy from New York became so interested in the evolution of monkeys. I hope that they would look favorably on the product of my efforts. In particular, I wish to thank my father, who has braved the devastating results of a major stroke for the past three years, for bringing home the books that sparked my interest in evolution and for suggesting that I apply to Penn for my undergraduate studies: both were seminal events.

Paul F. Whitehead
New Haven, CT

Contents

Bibliography is available on-line at http://www.morton-pub.com

CHAPTER ONE

Definition of the Primates

1

"The question of questions for mankind—the problem which underlines all others, and is more deeply interesting than any other—is the ascertainment of the place which Man occupies in nature and of his relations to the universe of things."

Thomas H. Huxley (1894)—*Man's Place in Nature*

"Even if it be granted that the difference between man and his nearest allies is as great in corporal structure as some naturalists maintain . . . the facts given in the earlier chapters appear to declare, in the plainest manner, that man is descended from some lower form . . ."

Charles Darwin (1871)—*The Descent of Man and Selection in Relation to Sex*

INTRODUCTION

Humans are members of the Order Primates, one of the number of orders that have evolved since the origin of the mammals in the Triassic. The structural affinities of humans to other primates was known even before Darwin presented the first comprehensive, modern paradigm of evolution in his *Origin of Species by Means of Natural Selection* in 1859. Linnaeus, in his classic *Systema Naturae,* first published in 1735, included humans in the Anthropomorpha (later called Primates) with lemurs, monkeys, and apes although he did not have a paradigm of evolution. We may therefore ask: What are the features that characterize primates in contrast to representatives of other orders of mammals?

However, we must first explore the features of primates that ally them to their closest relatives. That is, primates are *animals*, *chordates*, *vertebrates*, and *mammals*.

The term *animal* has a very specific meaning in biology. Animals, regardless of whether they are jellyfish, insects, fish, or humans, share certain defining characteristics. Animals can be defined as multicellular, heterotrophic, diploid organisms that develop from the union of two different haploid gametes, an "egg" (termed secondary oocyte in mammals) and a smaller sperm (Margulis and Schwartz, 1998). The cleavage divisions that follow fertilization produce a *blastula*, a hollow ball of cells; most animals (with the exception of the Porifera) are united by the presence of a blastula stage during embryonic development. Animals are not only multicellular—their cells are joined by *intercellular junctions* to form *tissues*. Most animals have ingestive nutrition, i.e., bulk food is taken into the organism and then digested.

Within the Animalia, primates belong to those subdivisions which have tissues organized into *organs* and *organ systems*, are *bilaterally symmetrical* (an anatomical arrangement in which the body is divided into mirror left and right halves along only one plane, usually midsagittal) and have a true body cavity (*coelem*) which is lined on all sides by the mesodermal lining termed *peritoneum*. Within the coelomates (eucoelomates), primates are animals in which the embryonic *blastopore* develops into the anus and so they are *deuterostomes*.

Within the deuterostomes, primates and other mammals belong to the *Chordata*. Chordates are defined by the presence of four important characteristics at some stage of their development, i.e., some characters are present during the embryonic stage only in certain taxa while they will persist into adulthood in other chordate taxa: the presence of a *notochord, gill slits in the throat (pharyngeal gill slits), a single dorsal hollow nerve chord* (which becomes the brain and spinal chord in humans and many other chordates), and a *postanal tail*. In addition, there are a number of other features to chordates, although they are not considered as defining: bilateral symmetry, segmented body organization including the presence of myomeres, complete digestive tract with a mouth and anus, sexual reproduction, separate sexes, and the presence of a ventral heart and closed circulatory system.

The Subphylum *Vertebrata* are those chordates in which vertebrae surround the spinal cord. The notocord is replaced by the bodies of the vertebrae. The cephalic portion of the dorsal hollow nerve chord develops into a brain which is enclosed in a protective skull (*cranium*). The vertebrates are further divided into the Agnatha, which consists today of the lampreys and hagfishes, and the *Gnathostomata*. The latter includes the primates, and is defined as the vertebrate superclass in which jaws are present, the notochord usually does not persist into adulthood, and appendages are generally paired.

The gnathostome vertebrates are divided into a number of classes, most of which are fishes. The *tetrapods* consist of the amphibians, reptiles, birds, and mammals. The mammals are comprised of the *Prototheria*, represented today only by the platypus and echidna, and the *Theria*. The latter contains two living infraclasses, *Metatheria* (pouched mammals or marsupials) and *Eutheria* (placental mammals).

MAMMALS

There are five major features that unite the mammals. Mammals have *hair*, although the relative amount differs significantly among taxa. Female mammals have *mammary glands* which produce milk for the nourishment of the young after birth. The middle ear of mammals possesses three tiny bones (ossicles): the *incus*, *malleus*, and *stapes*. Reptiles generally have only the stapes and they never have all three bones. There is only one bone in the lower jaw of a mammal, termed the *dentary*. Reptiles always have several bones in their lower jaws. The joint between the lower jaw and the remainder of the skull is formed between the dentary and *squamosal* (or between the dentary and the squamous portion of the temporal bone) in mammals. Other bones form the jaw joint in reptiles (Kardong, 1995). There are other features that characterize mammals as well (Table 1.1 and Figures 1.1, 1.2, and 1.3).

As eutherians, primates form a chorioallantoic placenta—a temporary organ formed from both fetal and maternal tissues that provides nutrients and oxygen to the fetus, carries away fetal wastes and produces the hormones of pregnancy. The placenta allows a lot of prenatal development to occur in the mother's uterus and eutherian young can be relatively large and advanced at birth. Prenatal development occurs more rapidly in the placental uterus than it does in the marsupial pouch (Carroll, 1988). In marsupials, the young are very immature at birth and have to continue their early development attached to a nipple in their mother's pouch (*marsupium*). It is asserted that the

TABLE 1.1 PRIMITIVE TRAITS OF EARLY PLACENTAL MAMMALS

Cranial			
	1) Carotid artery in medial position		21) Lacrimal-palatine contact extensive
	2) Occiput not posteriorly expanded		22) Lacrimal facial wing large
	3) Auditory bulla not ossified		23) Single lacrimal foramen exits par facialis
	4) Ectotympanic annular and inclined at an acute angle to the horizontal plane of the skull		24) Orbitosphenoid large
			25) Alisphenoid orbital wing small
	5) Jaw condyle distinctly lower than coronoid process	**Postcranial**	1) Scapula fossae narrow, shallow, subequal in area
	6) Postglenoid foramen retained		2) Manubrium of sternum not enlarged
	7) Origin of temporalis muscle extending anteriorly over frontal		3) Deltopectoral crest on humerus strong
	8) Palatal fenestrae absent		4) Entepicondylar foramen present
	9) Nasals broad posteriorly		5) Ulna robust, with sigmoid lateral curvature
	10) Infraorbital canal long		6) Pelvic-sacrum fusion limited
	11) Zygomatic arch complete, with large zygomatic bone (jugal)		7) Greater trochanter prominent, exceeding height of femoral head
	12) Postorbital process of frontal absent		8) Lesser trochanter large, lamelliform
	13) Anterior opening of alisphenoid canal confluent with foramen rotundum		9) Tibia-fibula broadly separate
	14) Supraorbital foramen absent		10) Distal elements of forelimbs and/or hindlimbs not markedly elongate
	15) Foramen rotundum confluent with sphenorbital foramen		11) Scaphoid and lunate unfused
	16) Optic foramen small		12) Os centrale present
	17) Suboptic foramen present		13) Metatarsals not greatly elongated
	18) Maxilla orbital wing small or absent		14) No metatarsals significantly reduced
	19) Fronto-maxillary contact absent		15) Calcaneal fibular facet pronounced
	20) Palatine orbital wing extensive		16) Superior astragular foramen present

placental strategy is to invest energy in intrauterine development of offspring but the marsupial strategy is to invest energy in postnatal development through lactation (Pough, Heiser, and McFarland, 1996). There are also skeletal differences between marsupial and placental mammals, many of which relate to the bones of the skull. For example, the optic foramen (for the passage of the optic nerve to the brain) usually runs through the orbitosphenoid in eutherians but it is joined to the anterior lacerate foramen as a space between the orbitosphenoid and alisphenoid in marsupials (Yapp, 1965). An obvious difference in the postcranial skeleton is that marsupials have epipubic bones on the pelvic girdle but eutherians do not (see Figure 1.4).

The number and relationships of orders of eutherians has historically been a matter of debate. For example, the "flying

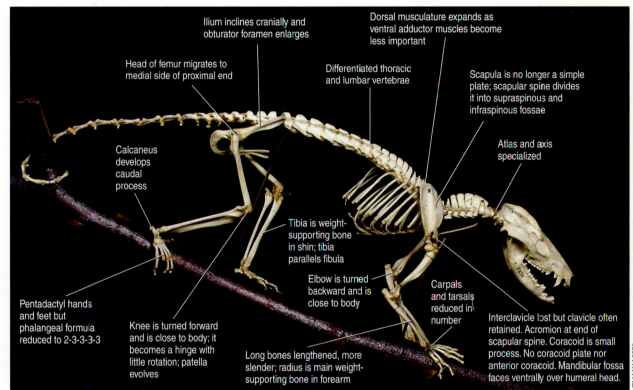

Ilium inclines cranially and obturator foramen enlarges

Dorsal musculature expands as ventral adductor muscles become less important

Head of femur migrates to medial side of proximal end

Differentiated thoracic and lumbar vertebrae

Scapula is no longer a simple plate; scapular spine divides it into supraspinous and infraspinous fossae

Calcaneus develops caudal process

Atlas and axis specialized

Tibia is weight-supporting bone in shin; tibia parallels fibula

Elbow is turned backward and is close to body

Carpals and tarsals reduced in number

Pentadactyl hands and feet but phalangeal formula reduced to 2-3-3-3-3

Knee is turned forward and is close to body; it becomes a hinge with little rotation; patella evolves

Long bones lengthened, more slender; radius is main weight-supporting bone in forearm

Interclavicle lost but clavicle often retained. Acromion at end of scapular spine. Coracoid is small process. No coracoid plate nor anterior coracoid. Mandibular fossa faces ventrally over humeral head.

YPM MAM 5270

1.1 Mounted skeleton of the marsupial Virginia opossum (*Didelphis virginiana*) illustrating general differences in the mammalian skeleton from those of contemporary reptiles.

Specimen courtesy of Yale Peabody Museum

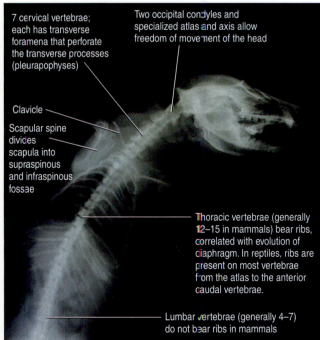

7 cervical vertebrae; each has transverse foramena that perforate the transverse processes (pleurapophyses)

Two occipital condyles and specialized atlas and axis allow freedom of movement of the head

Clavicle

Scapular spine divides scapula into supraspinous and infraspinous fossae

Thoracic vertebrae (generally 12–15 in mammals) bear ribs, correlated with evolution of diaphragm. In reptiles, ribs are present on most vertebrae from the atlas to the anterior caudal vertebrae.

Lumbar vertebrae (generally 4–7) do not bear ribs in mammals

1.2 Dorsal radiograph of an anaesthesized Virginia opossum, illustrating some general mammalian skeletal features.

Radiograph courtesy of Dr. Catherine Skinner

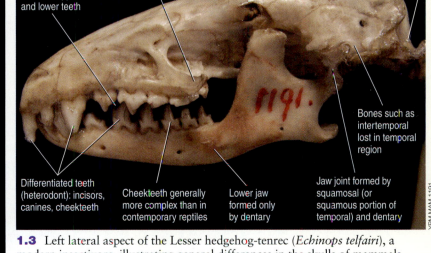

Circumorbital bones lost except for jugal and lacrimal

Enlarged braincase compared to body size, reflecting larger, more complex brain

Fusion of several bones to form complex bones such as temporal and occipital

Good occlusion between upper and lower teeth

Bones such as intertemporal lost in temporal region

Differentiated teeth (heterodont): incisors, canines, cheekteeth

Cheekteeth generally more complex than in contemporary reptiles

Lower jaw formed only by dentary

Jaw joint formed by squamosal (or squamous portion of temporal) and dentary

YPM MAM 1191

1.3 Left lateral aspect of the Lesser hedgehog-tenrec (*Echinops telfairi*), a modern insectivore, illustrating general differences in the skulls of mammals from those of modern reptiles.

Specimen courtesy of Yale Peabody Museum

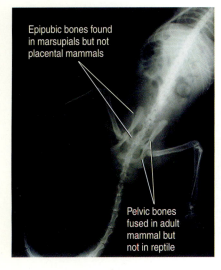

Epipubic bones found in marsupials but not placental mammals

Pelvic bones fused in adult mammal but not in reptile

1.4 Dorsal radiograph of the pelvic region of a Virginia opossum, illustrating the epipubic bones which differentiate marsupials from eutherian mammals. Also represented are some general mammalian postcranial features.

Radiograph courtesy of Dr. Catherine Skinner

lemurs" have generally been placed in their own order Dermoptera (Simpson, 1945; Yates, 1984) but Romer (1966) included them with the moles and shrews in the Insectivora. The treeshrews have been considered to be a Family (Tupaiidae) within the Insectivores (Vaughan, 1972) or a separate order of Mammals (Scandentia; Yates, 1984) or a superfamily (Tupaioidea) within the Primates (Clark, 1971:71).

Mammalogists have also debated whether there needs to be special recognition of phylogenetic relationship between various orders at a taxonomic level between the order and the subclass. The details of these discussions are beyond the scope of this atlas. Beard (1993) proposes that a mirorder be erected (Primatomorpha) as a monophyletic group to include the primates and dermopterans. Early in the 20th century, Gregory (1910) included four living orders in a group termed the Archonta—the elephant shrews, dermopterans, bats, and primates —which often is considered to be a superorder within the eutherians. Rasmussen (2002) and Rose (1995) add the Plesiadapiformes to the Archonta as an order separate from the Primates. As Thewissen and Babcock (1993:91) write, "There is little consensus concerning the internal relationships among the archontan taxa . . ." and Simmons (1993) presents a discussion

of this issue. A lot of the disagreement is related to the question of whether the plesiadapiforms, which have traditionally been considered to be primates (Clark, 1971; Simons, 1972; Szalay, 1969; Szalay and Delson, 1979), constitute a separate order (Rasmussen, 2002; Rose, 1995), are members of the order Dermoptera (Beard, 1993), or really are primates (Bloch and Silcox, 2001). Gingerich (1986) attempts to solve the problem by placing flying lemurs, treeshrews and plesiadapiforms in the "Praesimii", tarsiers, lemurs, and lorises in the "Prosimii" and monkeys, apes, and humans in the "Anthropoidea." Unfortunately, this approach groups species according to *grade* and not phylogenetically—a taboo in cladistic systematics.

INSECTIVORES

Anthropologists (Rose, Godinot and Bown, 1994; Szalay, 1969) have generally derived the primates from that group of mammals that are broadly termed *insectivores*. The insectivores are a very diverse group of eutherian mammals, sometimes divided into the Erinaceomorpha (hedgehogs), Soricomorpha (including moles and shrews), Tenrecomorpha (tenrecs), and Chrysochlorda (Golden mole) within the order Insectivora. They are also sometimes called the Lipotyphla ("lipotyphlan insectivores"). Carroll (1988:460) writes that they are often considered to be "among the most primitive living placentals" and details their primitive features: small brain, smooth cerebral hemispheres that do not expand over the cerebellum, some genera retain a cloaca, postorbital bar is absent, auditory bulla is rarely ossified, number and configuration of the teeth, plantigrade and pentadactyl hands and feet, and pollex and hallux not opposable. Most biologists think of insectivores in relation to their cheekteeth with high, pointed cusps that are well-adapted to piercing, cutting, and crushing their food. Carroll enumerates shared derived characters of the insectivores, based on Butler (1972) and Novacek (1980), including reduction or absence of the jugal and morphology of the medial wall of the orbit correlated with small eye size and a large nasal capsule. Figure 1.5 depicts some features of contemporary insectivores.

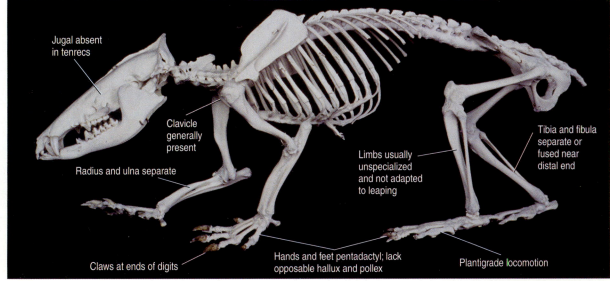

1.5 Mounted skeleton of a Lesser hedgehog-tenrec (*Echinops telfairi*), depicting some general skeletal features of insectivores.

Specimen courtesy of Yale Peabody Museum

Jugal absent in tenrecs

Clavicle generally present

Radius and ulna separate

Limbs usually unspecialized and not adapted to leaping

Tibia and fibula separate or fused near distal end

Claws at ends of digits

Hands and feet pentadactyl; lack opposable hallux and pollex

Plantigrade locomotion

YPM MAM 1192

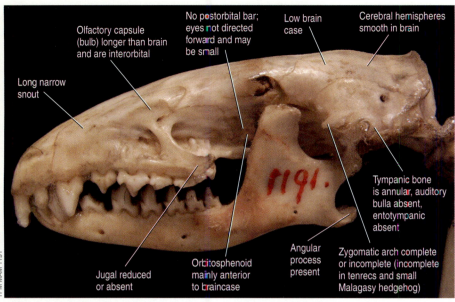

Olfactory capsule (bulb) longer than brain and are interorbital

No postorbital bar; eyes not directed forward and may be small

Low brain case

Cerebral hemispheres smooth in brain

Long narrow snout

Tympanic bone is annular, auditory bulla absent, entotympanic absent

Jugal reduced or absent

Orbitosphenoid mainly anterior to braincase

Angular process present

Zygomatic arch complete or incomplete (incomplete in tenrecs and small Malagasy hedgehog)

YPM MAM 1191

1.6 Left lateral aspect of Lesser hedgehog-tenrec, exemplifying general features of the skull in insectivores.
Specimen courtesy of Yale Peabody Museum

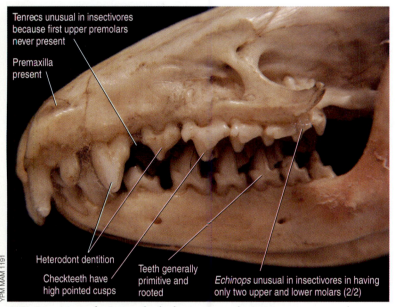

Tenrecs unusual in insectivores because first upper premolars never present

Premaxilla present

Heterodont dentition

Checkteeth have high pointed cusps

Teeth generally primitive and rooted

Echinops unusual in insectivores in having only two upper and lower molars (2/2)

YPM MAM 1191

1.7 Dentition of a Lesser hedgehog-tenrec, depicting some general features of the dentition of insectivores and some specializations of tenrecs.
Specimen courtesy of Yale Peabody Museum

There has been some suggestion that the primates may have originated from the Erinaceomorpha because of dental resemblances between early erinaceomorphs and the plesiadapiform *Purgatorius*, but this is controversial (Rose, Godinot, and Bown, 1994).

PRIMATE CHARACTERISTICS

Considering the controversy concerning the relationship of the primates to other mammals, it is fair for us to ask: What characters define a primate among the mammals? Unfortunately, the answer to this direct question has also been a matter of disagreement and various authors have used different criteria to define the primates. Hill (1972:1) writes "Primates differ from other mammals mainly in negative features, rendering more exact definition difficult and controversial" and Rasmussen (2002:5) echoes Simpson (1955) when he states that "Primates lack any one specialization that is as clear and unambiguous as the wing shared by all bats or the paddling tail of porpoises."

Many authors refer to the classic definition of the Primates by Mivart (1873), a definition considered by Hill (1972:1) to be ". . . adequate for general purposes . . .":

Unguiculate, claviculate placental mammals, with orbits encircled by bone; three kinds of teeth, at least at one time of life; brain always with a posterior lobe and calcarine fissure; the innermost digit of at least one pair of extremities opposable; hallux with a flattened nail or none; a well-developed caecum; penis pendulous; testes scrotal; always two pectoral mammae.

In their diagnosis of the primates, Thorington and Anderson (1984) identify four kinds of characters that have often been employed: retention of a *suite of primitive characters*, possession of a *suite of derived but not unique characters*, manifestation of a *suite of evolutionary trends*, and possession of *true synapomorphies* (Table 1.2). They also present some general characteristics (Table 1.3). While most other authors do not subdivide their lists of primate characteristics, aside from anatomical region of the body, most present some variation of the suite in Table 1.3. Notable examples include Clark (1971), Napier and Napier (1967), and Vallois (1955). In his recent discussion, Rasmussen (2002) focuses on a subset of the features discussed in Table 1.2: grasping hands and feet with opposable pollex and especially hallux, modification of claws into flat nails, eyes directed forward producing stereoscopic vision, larger brains than expected for their sizes, single births and slow development, and an auditory bulla formed from the petrosal bone.

The almost universal application of cladistic (Hennig, 1966) methodology and theory to systematics has led to a challenge of the way in which anthropologists define the primates and identify whether particular forms (e.g., treeshrews, plesiadapiforms) should be considered primates. Martin (1986:2) states that, while solely descriptive definitions can include both primitive (*plesiomorphic*, e.g., pentadactyly) and derived (*apomorphic*, e.g., auditory bulla covered by petrosal) characters, ". . . definitions intended for phylogenetic reconstruction should include only inferred derived character states . . ." In his discussion of primate characteristics, he includes both unique features and character states that occur in other orders of mammals Table 1.4. Unlike some earlier authors, Martin (1986) states that reduction of the olfactory apparatus has occurred only in diurnal primate species.

TABLE 1.2 CHARACTERS USED TO DIAGNOSE THE PRIMATES BY THORINGTON AND ANDERSON (1984)

TYPE OF CHARACTER	STATE FOUND IN PRIMATES	TYPE OF CHARACTER	STATE FOUND IN PRIMATES

Primitive	1) Eutherian mammal.
	2) Generalized limbs:
	  a) usually pentadactyl
	  b) unfused radius and ulna
	  c) presence of a clavicle
	  d) unfused scaphoid and lunate
	  e) commonly have os centrale
	  f) tibia and fibula usually unfused
	3) Heterodont and diphyodont dentition.
		Derived But Not Unique (cont)	3) Complete postorbital bar (except in plesiadapiforms).
			4) Calcarine and retrocalcarine sulci present.

		Evolutionary Trends	1) Reducing nose and sense of smell. 2) Enlarging eyes and improving vision. 3) Enlarging brain (especially cerebral cortex). 4) Progressively improving placentation.
Derived But Not Unique	1) Hallux bears flat nail and is usually opposable. 2) Other digits bear nails that range from flat to vaulted to clawlike.	True Synapomorphies	Petrosal-covered auditory bulla with tympanic floor derived only from petrosal plate and ectotympanic.

TABLE 1.3 GENERAL CHARACTERISTICS OF PRIMATES ACCORDING TO THORINGTON AND ANDERSON (1984)

Behavioral	1) Mostly arboreal 2) Phytophagous 3) Omnivorous (rarely insectivorous or carnivorous)
Dental	1) Permanent dentition of 18–36 teeth: I^{0-2}/I_{1-2}, C^{0-1}/C_{0-1}, P^{2-4}/P_{2-4}, M^{2-3}/M_{2-3}. 2) Incisors in some cases reduced or lost (upper incisors in some lemurs) 3) Incisors in some cases enlarged (rodentlike in *Daubentonia*) or otherwise specialized (lower incisors of dental comb in Recent lemurs, of *Tarsius* and of some extinct forms) 4) Premolars reduced to 3 or fewer in all recent taxa, typically bicuspid, rarely caniniform (e.g., *Indri*, *Propithecus*) or tending toward molariform 5) Molars bearing 3, 4, or 5 cusps, primitively brachydont and tuberculosectorial but becoming more bunodont in "advanced" groups
Cranial	1) Jaw movement mainly vertical [Hiiemae (2000:224) describes some transverse movement in macaques] 2) Mandibular symphysis firmly ossified in "advanced groups" 3) Orbits more or less directed forward 4) Orbits separated from temporal fossa by postorbital bar or plate (except in *Plesiadapis*) 5) Only 3 or 4 ethmoturbinals 6) Braincase becoming relatively large and facial region relatively small except in some lemurs and baboons
Brain and Sensory	1) Nasal region progressively enlarged and elaborated 2) Brain progressively enlarged and elaborated 3) Cerebrum primitively smooth and not covering cerebellum but hemispheres and especially neopallium expanded in "higher" groups, richly convoluted and covering cerebellum
Digestive	1) Liver lobate 2) Gallbladder present 3) Stomach simple except in leaf-eating colobines 4) Duodenojejunal flexure present 5) Cecum present
Reproductive	1) Uterus bicornate or simplex 2) Placenta non-deciduous and diffuse or deciduous and discoidal 3) Penis not enclosed in a sheath bound to body wall, distally more or less free and often pendulous, but scarcely projecting in some marmosets 4) Testes extra-abdominal, either scrotal or subintegumental, and postpenial, prepenial (some gibbons) or parapenial (some marmosets) 5) Baculum usually present except in *Tarsius*, some New World monkeys and *Homo*

TABLE 1.4 CHARACTERS OF THE PRIMATES ACCORDING TO MARTIN (1986)

Geographical Distribution and Habitat Occupancy	1) Tropical/subtropical forest ecosystems. 2) Arboreal.
Locomotor Adaptations	*1) Grasping foot with well-developed, divergent hallux. *2) Tarsi-fulcruminating foot. 3) Calcaneus in contact with navicular. *4) Pronounced elongation of the distal segment of the calcaneus; calcaneal index value is less than 100%. *5) Hindlimb domination, reflected by greater proportion of body weight borne by hindlimbs and diagonal sequence gait. 6) Some prehensile capacity in hand. 7) Flat nails on digits, at least on hallux. 8) Tactile pads with dermatoglyphs (ridges) and Meissner's corpuscles (touch).
Major Sense Organs and Skull Morphology	1) Large orbits relative to skull length. 2) Postorbital bar. *3) Pronounced degree of forward rotation of the orbits, relative to skull size and reduction of the interorbital breadth. 4) Exposure of the ethmoid bone as a flat plate in the medial wall of the orbit. *5) Neural specialization for effective stereoscopic vision: Partial cross-over of optic tracts. *6) Inputs to both eyes from the right half of the binocular field pass exclusively to the left half of the brain and vice versa. *7) Petrosal bone forms ventral floor of auditory bulla.
Brain	1) Relatively larger brains than many other mammals. *2) True Sylvan sulcus confluent with rhinal sulcus. *3) Calcarine sulcus that is three-branched (triradiate). *4) Fetal brain size large relative to fetal body size.
Reproductive Biology	*1) Males have permanent descent of testes into a post-penial scrotum; descent occurs close to time of birth. 2) Loss of urogenital sinus in females, so urethra and vagina have separate external meatae. 3) Early vascularization of chorion by allantoic vessels and reduction of involvement of yolk sac in placentation during the latter part of gestation. 4) Gestation period long relative to body size. 5) Produce small litters of precocial neonates. 6) Maximum of three pairs of teats in females. 7) Pace of fetal and postnatal growth are slow relative to maternal body size and primate attain sexual maturity late and have long life spans.
Dental Patterns	1) Less change in reduction of the number of teeth and in the complexity of crown morphology of cheekteeth than in other orders. 2) Maximum dental formula is I2/2, C1/1, P3/3, M3/3 with loss of at least one incisor and one premolar from each toothrow compared to inferred ancestral dental formula for placental mammals. 3) Reduction in size of premaxilla and transverse arrangement of upper incisors. 4) Cheekteeth relatively unspecialized with relatively low, rounded cusp morphology and large, raised talonid basins on lower molars.

*Character state is unique to the order Primates.

Carolina Gray Squirrel (Rodentia) Compared to Capuchin Monkey (Primates)

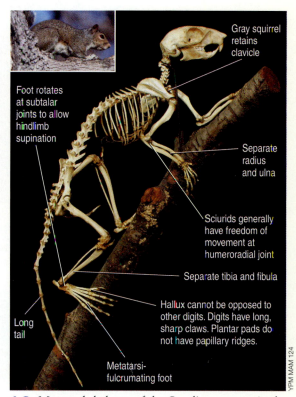

Gray squirrel retains clavicle

Foot rotates at subtalar joints to allow hindlimb supination

Separate radius and ulna

Sciurids generally have freedom of movement at humeroradial joint

Separate tibia and fibula

Hallux cannot be opposed to other digits. Digits have long, sharp claws. Plantar pads do not have papillary ridges.

Long tail

Metatarsi-fulcrumating foot

YPM MAM 124

1.8 Mounted skeleton of the Carolina gray squirrel (*Sciurus carolinensi*s), an arboreal/semiterrestrial rodent.   Specimen courtesy of Yale Peabody Museum
Inset photo courtesy of Bill Sacco

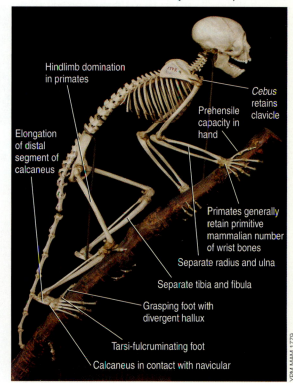

Hindlimb domination in primates

Cebus retains clavicle

Prehensile capacity in hand

Elongation of distal segment of calcaneus

Primates generally retain primitive mammalian number of wrist bones

Separate radius and ulna

Separate tibia and fibula

Grasping foot with divergent hallux

Tarsi-fulcruminating foot

Calcaneus in contact with navicular

YPM MAM 1779

1.9 Mounted skeleton of a White-headed capuchin monkey (*Cebus capucinus*).

Specimen courtesy of Yale Peabody Museum

Comparisons of Skulls of Gray Squirrel (Rodentia), Ring-tailed lemur (Primates), and Capuchin Monkey (Primates)

1.10 Skull of a Carolina gray squirrel (*Sciurus carolinensis*). **A** Left lateral view. **B** Frontal view. Squirrels are sciuromorph rodents, generally considered to be "more primitive" in their skull morphology than are other types of rodents.

Specimen courtesy of Yale Peabody Museum

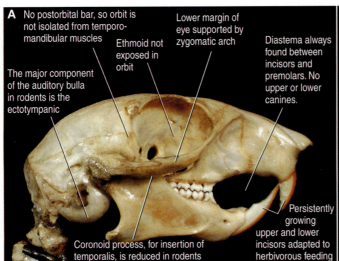

A No postorbital bar, so orbit is not isolated from temporo-mandibular muscles

The major component of the auditory bulla in rodents is the ectotympanic

Ethmoid not exposed in orbit

Lower margin of eye supported by zygomatic arch

Diastema always found between incisors and premolars. No upper or lower canines.

Coronoid process, for insertion of temporalis, is reduced in rodents

Persistently growing upper and lower incisors adapted to herbivorous feeding

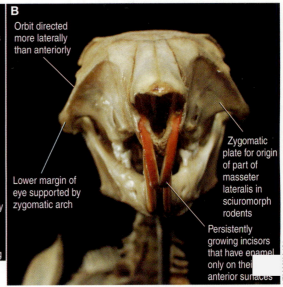

B Orbit directed more laterally than anteriorly

Lower margin of eye supported by zygomatic arch

Zygomatic plate for origin of part of masseter lateralis in sciuromorph rodents

Persistently growing incisors that have enamel only on their anterior surfaces

YPM MAM 124

1.11 Ring-tailed lemur skull. **A** Left lateral view. **B** Frontal view. Ring-tailed lemurs are strepsirhine primates.

Specimen courtesy of Yale Peabody Museum

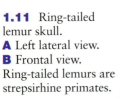

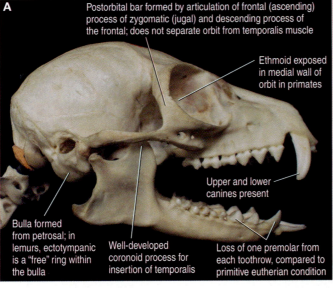

A Postorbital bar formed by articulation of frontal (ascending) process of zygomatic (jugal) and descending process of the frontal; does not separate orbit from temporalis muscle

Ethmoid exposed in medial wall of orbit in primates

Bulla formed from petrosal; in lemurs, ectotympanic is a "free" ring within the bulla

Well-developed coronoid process for insertion of temporalis

Upper and lower canines present

Loss of one premolar from each toothrow, compared to primitive eutherian condition

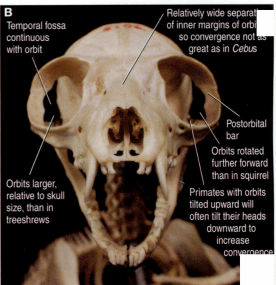

B Temporal fossa continuous with orbit

Relatively wide separat of inner margins of orbi so convergence not as great as in *Cebus*

Postorbital bar

Orbits rotated further forward than in squirrel

Orbits larger, relative to skull size, than in treeshrews

Primates with orbits tilted upward will often tilt their heads downward to increase convergence

YPM MAM 5106

1.12 White-headed capuchin monkey skull. **A** Left lateral view. **B** Frontal view. Capuchin monkeys are haplorhine primates.

Specimen courtesy of Yale Peabody Museum

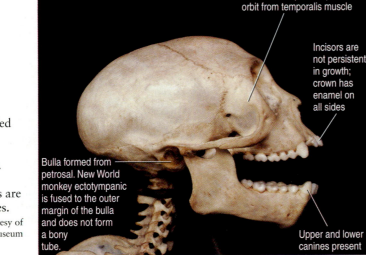

A Postorbital septum separates orbit from temporalis muscle

Incisors are not persistent in growth; crown has enamel on all sides

Bulla formed from petrosal. New World monkey ectotympanic is fused to the outer margin of the bulla and does not form a bony tube.

Upper and lower canines present

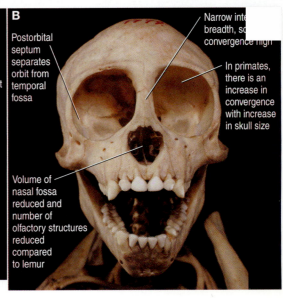

B Narrow inte breadth, s convergence high

Postorbital septum separates orbit from temporal fossa

In primates, there is an increase in convergence with increase in skull size

Volume of nasal fossa reduced and number of olfactory structures reduced compared to lemur

YPM MAM 1779

Dentition in Two Non-Primate Orders of Mammals

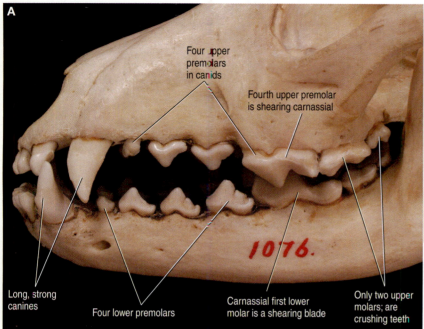

A

Four upper premolars in canids

Fourth upper premolar is shearing carnassial

Long, strong canines

Four lower premolars

Carnassial first lower molar is a shearing blade

Only two upper molars; are crushing teeth

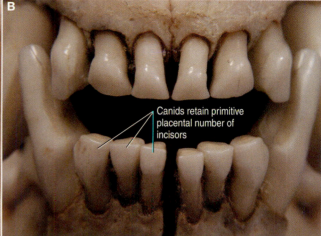

B

Canids retain primitive placental number of incisors

YPM MAM 1076

1.13 Dentition in a Golden jackal (*Canis aureus*), an Old World canid species distributed from Senegal to Thailand and Sri Lanka. **A** Left lateral view. **B** Frontal view. Jackals, wolves, dogs and foxes are canids—members of the order Carnivora. Teeth of carnivores are unlike those of primates in that the fourth upper premolar and first lower molar are specialized shearing blades called *carnassials*. In dogs (1.13a), the fourth upper premolar has a single cutting edge with protocone, paracone, and metacone; the first lower molar has shearing blade with paraconid, metaconid, and talonid (heel). Dogs are less specialized than cats in their teeth, in that they retain at least two post-carnassial grinding molars. Primates never have specialized carnassial cheekteeth. In contrast, canids retain the primitive mammalian number of incisors (1.13b).   Specimen courtesy of Yale Peabody Museum

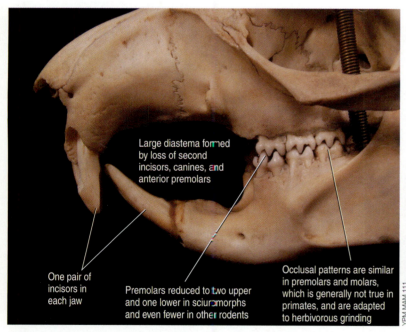

Large diastema formed by loss of second incisors, canines, and anterior premolars

One pair of incisors in each jaw

Premolars reduced to two upper and one lower in sciuromorphs and even fewer in other rodents

Occlusal patterns are similar in premolars and molars, which is generally not true in primates, and are adapted to herbivorous grinding

YPM MAM 111

1.14 Left lateral aspect of the occluded dentition of a marmot (*Marmota monax*), a sciuromorph rodent. Rodents are characterized by possessing only one pair of incisors in each jaw, loss of the second incisors, canines, and anterior premolars. The molars manifest the original eutherian pattern of cusps in squirrels but they are arranged in transverse rows, with the paracone and protocone mesially and metacone and hypocone distally (Young, 1981). Transverse ridges connect the cusps (*bilophodont*). Other rodents have even more elaborate, *multilophodont*, occlusal surfaces on molars. The teeth are also high-crowned (*hypsodont*) and grow continually.
Specimen courtesy of Yale Peabody Museum

Auditory Bulla in Primates

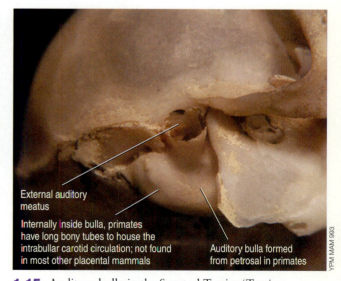

External auditory meatus

Internally inside bulla, primates have long bony tubes to house the intrabullar carotid circulation; not found in most other placental mammals

Auditory bulla formed from petrosal in primates

YPM MAM 993

1.15 Auditory bulla in the Spectral Tarsier (*Tarsius spectrum*). The petrosal is the major bulla element in primates. Other bones form the bulla in other mammalian orders, such as the ectotympanic in rodents, lagomorphs, proboscidea, artiodactyls, perrissodactyls, cetaceans, and some carnivores. The primitive condition in mammals was an unossified auditory bulla.

Specimen courtesy of Yale Peabody Museum

Parental Care and Extended Juvenile Period in Primates

1.16 Adult female Golden langur (*Trachypithecus [Presbytis] geei*) and her son. Primates typically manifest considerable maternal care of their offspring. Primates also generally show a long juvenile period (for their body size) before sexual maturity, which is related to one of their fundamental adaptive strategies—individual learning.

Photo courtesy of
Dr. Thomas T. Struhsaker

Grasping Foot of Primates

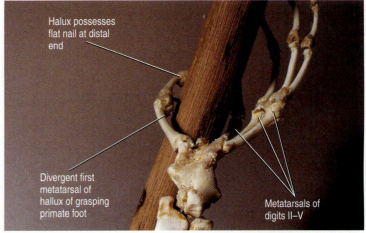

Halux possesses flat nail at distal end

Divergent first metatarsal of hallux of grasping primate foot

Metatarsals of digits II–V

1.17 Grasping foot in an adult howler monkey (*Alouatta*). The possession of a long, mobile hallux is considered to be part of the ancestral primate morphotype and Cartmill (1974:50) argues that "The danger of falling [in an arboreal mammal] is reduced if the animal can keep a firm grip on the support behind while testing the one ahead. Therefore, the grasping ability of the hind foot is more important in locomotion than that of the hand, and the hallux is accordingly more divergent than the pollex in the majority of arboreal mammals having grasping extremities."

Specimen courtesy of Yale Peabody Museum

Reduction of Elements in the Hands or Feet of Other Mammals

Sciurids generally have freedom of movement at wrist joints but scaphoid and lunate are fused in hands of squirrels and treeshrews

Thumb is reduced and cannot be opposed to other digits around a support

Metacarpals are always adducted

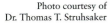

1.18 Hand of a gray squirrel.

Specimen courtesy of Yale Peabody Museum

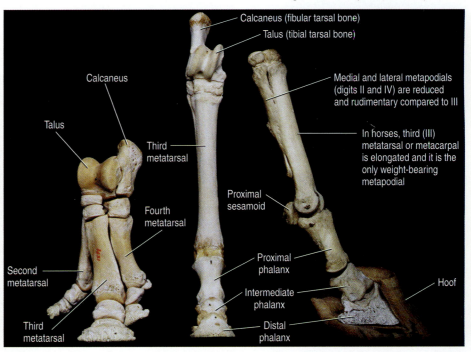

Calcaneus (fibular tarsal bone)

Talus (tibial tarsal bone)

Calcaneus

Talus

Third metatarsal

Fourth metatarsal

Second metatarsal

Third metatarsal

Medial and lateral metapodials (digits II and IV) are reduced and rudimentary compared to III

In horses, third (III) metatarsal or metacarpal is elongated and it is the only weight-bearing metapodial

Proximal sesamoid

Proximal phalanx

Intermediate phalanx

Distal phalanx

Hoof

1.19 Illustration of tapir and horse limbs showing the reduction of the number of digital elements in perissodactyls. About one-third of mammalian genera are herbivores and more than half of these are artiodactyls (even toed) and perissodactyls (odd-toed). The latter (tapirs, horses, and rhinos) generally have one to three digits while the former (including pigs, camels, antelopes, deer, giraffe, and cattle) have two to four digits. The ancestral mammalian morphotype had five toes/fingers on each appendage. In both perissodactyls and artiodactyls, the limbs tended to become long, many show digitigrady or unguligrady and the number of digits were reduced during evolution. "These modifications, combined with alterations in the ankle joints and fusion of paired limb bones, enabled the herbivores to exploit fully a vast array of terrains, move efficiently over long migrations and rapidly escape predators" (Savage and Long, 1986:188). These specializations are very different from the more generalized, arboreally adapted skeleton of most primates.

Photograph courtesy of Bill Sacco

Nails Versus Claws

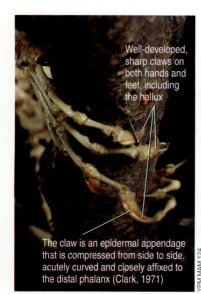

Well-developed, sharp claws on both hands and feet, including the hallux

The claw is an epidermal appendage that is compressed from side to side, acutely curved and closely affixed to the distal phalanx (Clark, 1971)

YPM MAM 124

1.20 Hand in the Carolina gray squirrel. Cartmill (1974:76) writes that, "On tree trunks and other nonhorizontal supports of relatively large diameter, claw grip is demonstrably superior to pad grip."

Specimen courtesy of Yale Peabody Museum

Distal phalanges do not bear claws. Primate digits generally have terminal pads which are highly sensitive to touch.

Distal phalanx does not have the curved, claw-like shape of clawed mammals

Clark (1971:173) argues that hands with pads rather than claws permit primates to hold "with much more precision surfaces of varying shape, size, and texture."

YPM MAM 1779

1.21 Hand in a capuchin monkey.

Specimen courtesy of Yale Peabody Museum

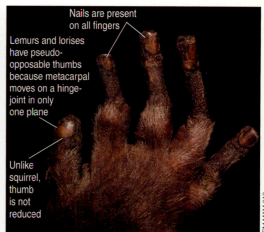

Nails are present on all fingers

Lemurs and lorises have pseudo-opposable thumbs because metacarpal moves on a hinge-joint in only one plane

Unlike squirrel, thumb is not reduced

YPM MAM 318

1.22 Hand in a mounted Northern Greater Galago (*Otolemur garnetti*). Primates generally have nails on their fingers and toes rather than claws and possess pads on the palmar surfaces of their hands and the plantar surfaces of their feet. See Cartmill (1974) for a thorough discussion of the relative advantages of pads versus claws in arboreal locomotion.

Specimen courtesy of Yale Peabody Museum

Nails are present on all fingers

1.23 Hand of a mounted howler monkey (*Alouatta*), depicting its nails.

Specimen courtesy of Yale Peabody Museum

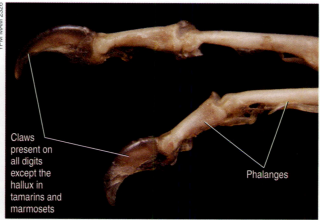

YPM MAM 2326

Claws present on all digits except the hallux in tamarins and marmosets

Phalanges

1.24 Claws of a Cottontop tamarin (*Saguinus oedipus*). Marmosets and tamarins are descended from an ancestor that "re-evolved" claws, as the possession of nails is part of the ancestral primate morphotype. Cartmill (1974:58) writes that the claws of marmosets and tamarins "facilitate several squirrel-like locomotor habits, including running spirally up and down tree trunks." The possession of claws also facilitates their access to gum or sap from broad vertical arboreal supports.

Specimen courtesy of Yale Peabody Museum

YPM MAM 2326

1.25 Palmar aspect of the inside of a claw of a Cottontop tamarin (*Saguinus oedipus*), depicting the groove on the undersurface. Clark (1971) writes that the groove is relatively wider than in treeshrews and the claw is not as compressed from side-to-side.

Specimen courtesy of Yale Peabody Museum

1.26 Claws of an aye-aye (*Daubentonia madagascariensis*). An aye-aye has claws rather than nails on all digits other than its hallux. Claws would facilitate access to vertical supports during their feeding on wood-boring insect larvae. Again, this is a situation where this species is presumably descended from an ancestor that "re-evolved" claws because of the particular ecological niche to which is was adapted.

Specimen courtesy of Yale Peabody Museum

YPM MAM 919

Clavicle

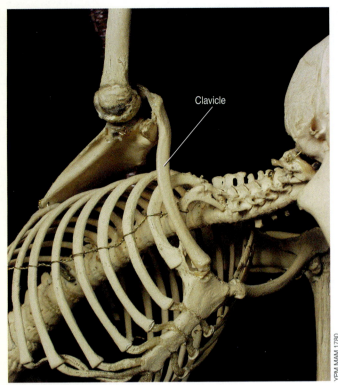

YPM MAM 1780

1.27 Right clavicle of a gibbon (*Hylobates*). Primates are characterized by possessing a *clavicle* as part of their pectoral girdle. The clavicle is a bone which articulates the sternum with the acromion process of the scapula. The clavicle serves as an attachment area for muscles such as deltoid and pectoralis major. It also serves to position the joint between the scapula and humerus away from the ribcage, thus allowing greater freedom of movement at the shoulder. Many other mammals that engage in arboreal locomotor behaviors also possess clavicle such as the Virginia opossum (Figure 1.2) and Gray squirrel (Figure 1.8).   Specimen courtesy of Yale Peabody Museum

Arboreal Hypothesis

What selective forces account for the possession of these characteristics? Anthropologists have tended to focus on features related to locomotion, senses, and intelligence. The most influential explanation for the possession of features such as pentadactyl hands and feet, abducted hallux and pollex, free mobility of the forelimb and hindlimb with unfused radius and fibula, forward-directed orbits, and the presence of nails and friction pads has been Wood Jones's (1916:13) interpretation that they are adaptations to arboreal life: ". . . what was the factor that saved the particular mammalian stock which culminated in Man from becoming four-footed pronogrades? We will answer by saying at once, "The arboreal habit.'" Adaptation to arboreality has also been interpreted as the cause of reduction in the sense of smell and increased emphasis on vision (Grafton Elliot Smith quoted in Hooton, 1946:72):

Once such a creature left the solid earth and took to an arboreal life . . . the guidance of the olfactory sense lost much of its usefulness. Life amidst the branches of the trees limits the usefulness of the olfactory organs, but it is favorable to the high development of vision, touch and hearing.

The "arboreal hypothesis" was adapted by a variety of authors, spanning decades (e.g., Campbell, 1988; Hooton, 1940).

Cartmill (1974) presents a modification of the arboreal hypothesis that may be termed the "visual predation hypothesis." He argues that adaptation to living in the arboreal milieu *per se* is not the explanation for the suite of primate features because many other taxa of mammals manifest other features (e.g., squirrels have claws rather than nails, arboreal sloths do not grasp branches by the use of a broadly divergent, opposable pollex but volarflex hand claws against a pad) that allow them to be highly successful in arboreal positional behaviors. Instead, he compares primate adaptations to those of small arboreal marsupials and concludes that they are similar to those species that ". . . stalk and manually seize insect prey among the slender branches of bushes and low trees of tropical forests and woodlands" and concludes "Reduction of claws and development of grasping specializations of the hand have occurred independently, in different ways and for different reasons, in various primate lineages" (Cartmill, 1974:76). He points-out that modern *Loris*, *Galago*, and *Tarsius* feed in this manner. So, it may be that the origin of the primates can be explained by adaptation to a *particular arboreal niche*. In fairness to Wood Jones, he (1916:18) did say that "The arboreal habit alone is not the talisman; other mammalian stocks have taken to an arboreal habit . . ." although he argued that primates were more "perfect" in their adaptation to the arboreal milieu—a terminology that modern evolutionary biologists would not employ.

1.28 Vertical clinging of an adult female Coquerel's Sifaka (*Propithecus coquereli*) and her son. This species is found in north-western Madagascar.

Photo courtesy of Dr. Thomas T. Struhsaker

1.29 Descent down a tree trunk in a wild Zanzibar bushbaby (*Galago zanzibaricus*). This species is a vertical clinger and leaper that lives in coastal forests from southern Somalia to Central Tanzania and Zanzibar Island. The animal's eyes appear to be shining because of the possession of a tapetum lucidum. This is an area between the retina (nervous tunic) and choroid (vascular tunic) of the eyeball which reflects light through the retina. It is usually interpreted as an adaptation to vision in dim light conditions (Martin, 1990) and is considered to be part of the ancestral primate morphotype. Martin (1990) reviews the occurrence of the tapetum in different species of primates. The galago also has large, mobile ears—part of the ancestral primate morphotype.

Photo courtesy of Dr. Thomas T. Struhsaker

| TABLE 1.5 CLASSIFICATION OF STREPSIRHINE POSITIONAL BEHAVIOR* |||
CATEGORY	DEFINITION	TAXA
Active Quadrupedalism	These animals are primarily rapid, arboreal quadrupedal runners and climbers, although some are fairly proficient leapers. They are all capable of some vertical climbing.	Lemuridae *Eulemur, Varecia* Cheirogaleidae *Cheirogaleus, Microcebus, Phaner* Daubentoniidae *Daubentonia* Galagonidae *Otolemur crassicaudatus*
Slow-climbing Quadrupedalism	These animals are all slow and cautious arboreal climbers that rely on bridging behaviors rather than leaping in order to cross gaps in the forest canopy. They use suspensory movements more than any other strepsirrhines.	Loridae *Loris, Nycticebus, Arctocebus, Perodicticus*
Vertical Clinging and Leaping **	These rapid saltatorial animals usually rely on leaping to cross gaps in the forest, may preferentially use vertical supports during postural and locomotor behavior, and are often bipedal hoppers on the ground. Extensive variation exists within this group in the amount of leaping and quadrupedalism utilized, and in the size and orientation of preferred supports.	Galagonidae *Galago* Indridae *Indri, Avahi, Propithecus* Lemuridae *Hapalemur* Megaladapidae *Lepilemur*

*Family taxonomy modified to be consistent with Groves, 2001.

**Anemone's (1993) original table includes tarsiers in the Vertical Clinging and Leaping category because it was a table of positional behavior in "prosimians" rather than in strepsirrhines.

From *Postcranial Adaptation in Nonhuman Primates* by Daniel Gebo, p. 159. Copyright © 1993. Used by permission of Northern Illinois University Press.

PRIMATE SYSTEMATICS

It is impossible to speak of the objects of any study, or to think lucidly about them, unless they are named. It is impossible to examine their relationships to each other and their places among the vast, incredibly complex phenomena of the universe, in short to treat them scientifically, without putting them into some sort of formal arrangement.

George Gaylord Simpson (1945)
The Principles of Classification and a Classification of the Mammals

After a number of years of relative quiescence, except for the naming of fossil species and discussion of their affinities, primate taxonomy has experienced a renaissance. The renewal of interest has been ignited by the widespread application of molecular techniques (Disotell, 2000) and of cladistic philosophy and methodology (Groves, 2000, 2001).

After the publication of Simpson's (1945) classic taxonomy of the mammals (Table 1.6), physical anthropologists (e.g., Genet-Varcin, 1963; Simons, 1972) generally viewed both living and fossil primates in the framework of two suborders: Prosimii and Anthropoidea. The former consisted of the treeshrews,

1.30 Ascent up a vertical branch in a Mongoose lemur (*Eulemur mongoz*). Mongoose lemurs are found on Madagascar. Lemurs are basically quadrupedal primates although they do engage in leaping behaviors. They do not have the specialized anatomy that is found in vertical clinging and leaping species such as tarsiers, sifakas and bushbabies.   Photo courtesy of Dr. Thomas T. Struhsaker

lemurs, lorises, and tarsiers. The latter of the New World monkeys, Old World monkeys, apes, and humans. Within the Anthropoidea, the greater and lesser apes (Pongidae) were separated at the family level from humans (Hominidae) (Table 1.7). The paradigm had a temporal aspect to it, i.e., animals that possessed "prosimian" features appeared earlier in the fossil record than animals with "anthropoid" features and animals with "ape" features appeared earlier than did those with "human" features. It also had a gradistic aspect to it, as evidenced by Hill's (1972) "developmental evolutionary horizons": monkeys were considered to be more advanced than lemurs and humans more advanced than apes.

Strepsirhine Versus Haplorhine

Groves (2001) follows the precedent set by Pocock (1918) by dividing the primates into the two suborders Strepsirrhini (lemurs, lorises, and galagos) and Haplorrhini (tarisers, monkeys, apes, and humans) rather than Prosimii and Anthropoidea. (Note that many other authors spell these two taxonomic groups Strepsirhini and Haplorhini.) In the cladistic taxonomic framework, it is suggested that the Strepsirrhini and the Haplorrhini are both monophyletic groups—which would be preferable to the gradistic classification of "prosimians" and "anthropoids" of Simpson (1945). The basic defining difference is that strepsirhines have a nasal rhinarium while haplorhines do not (Figures 1.31, 1.32, and 1.33). Other characteristics of strepsirhines include

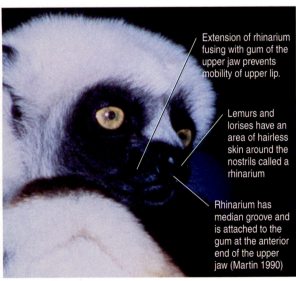

Extension of rhinarium fusing with gum of the upper jaw prevents mobility of upper lip.

Lemurs and lorises have an area of hairless skin around the nostrils called a rhinarium

Rhinarium has median groove and is attached to the gum at the anterior end of the upper jaw (Martin 1990)

1.31 Adult female Verreaux's sifaka. Lemurs, galagos, and lorises possess an area of moist, glandular and almost hairless skin surrounding the nostrils called the *rhinarium* (Martin, 1990). They are, therefore, termed *strepsirhines*. Note the well-developed snout. The presence of a rhinarium is common in many orders of mammals and is considered to be part of the ancestral primate morphotype. Photo courtesy of Dr. Thomas T. Struhsaker

TABLE 1.6A TRADITIONAL CLASSIFICATION OF THE PRIMATES ACCORDING TO SIMPSON (1945): SUBORDERS, INFRAORDERS, SUPERFAMILIES, AND FAMILIES OF LIVING PRIMATES

SUBORDER	INFRAORDER	SUPERFAMILY	FAMILY
Prosimii Illiger, 1811	Lemuriformes Gregory, 1915	Tupaioidea Dobson, 1882	Anagalidae Simpson, 1931
			Tupaiidae Mivart, 1868
		Lemuroidea Mivart, 1864	Lemuridae Gray, 1821
			Indridae Burnett, 1828
		Daubentonioidea Gill, 1872	Daubentoniidae Gray, 1870
	Lorisiformes Gregory, 1915		Lorisidae Gregory, 1915
	Tarsiiformes Gregory, 1915		Tarsiidae Gill, 1872
Anthropoidea Mivart, 1864		Ceboidea Simpson, 1931	Cebidae Swainson, 1835
			Callithricidae Thomas, 1903
		Cercopithecoidea Simpson, 1931	Cercopithecidae Gray, 1821
		Hominoidea Simpson, 1931	Pongidae Elliot, 1913
			Hominidae Gray, 1825

Used by permission of the American Museum of Natural History, New York, NY.

TABLE 1.6B TRADITIONAL CLASSIFICATION OF THE PRIMATES ACCORDING TO SIMPSON (1945): FAMILIES, SUBFAMILIES, AND GENERA

FAMILY	SUBFAMILY	GENERA
Anagalidae Simpson, 1931		*Anagale* Simpson, 1931
Tupaiidae Mivart, 1868	Tupaiinae Lyon, 1913	*Tupaia* Raffles, 1822 *Anathana* Lyon, 1913 *Dendrogale* Gray, 1848 *Tana* Lyon, 1913 *Urogale* Mearns, 1905
	Ptilocercinae Lyon, 1913	*Ptilocercus* Gray, 1848
Lemuridae Gray, 1821	Lemurinae Mivart, 1864	*Hapalemur* Geoffroy, 1851 *Lemur* Linnaeus, 1758 *Lepilemur* Geoffroy, 1851
	Cheirogaleinae Gregory, 1915	*Cheirogaleus* Geoffroy, 1812 *Microcebus* Geoffory, 1828 *Phaner* Gray, 1870

Continued

TABLE 1.6B TRADITIONAL CLASSIFICATION OF THE PRIMATES ACCORDING TO SIMPSON (1945): FAMILIES, SUBFAMILIES AND GENERA (continued)

FAMILY	SUBFAMILY	GENERA
Indridae Burnett, 1828		*Lichanotus* Illiger, 1811 *Propithecus* Bennett, 1832 *Indri* Geoffory, 1796
Daubentoniidae Gray, 1870		*Daubentonia* Geoffroy, 1795
Lorisidae Gregory, 1915	Lorisinae Flower and Lydekker, 1891	*Loris* Geoffroy, 1796 *Nycticebus* Geoffroy, 1812 *Arctocebus* Gray, 1863 *Perodicticus* Bennett, 1831
	Galaginae Mivart, 1864	*Galago* Geoffroy, 1796 *Euoticus* Gray, 1863
Tarsiidae Gill, 1872		*Tarsius* Starr, 1780
Cebidae Swainson, 1835	Aotinae Elliot, 1913	*Aotes* Humboldt, 1811 *Callicebus* Thomas, 1903
	Pitheciinae Mivart, 1865	*Cacajao* Lesson, 1840 *Pithecia* Desmarest, 1804 *Chiropotes* Lesson, 1840
	Alouattinae Elliot, 1904	*Alouatta* Lacepede, 1799
	Cebinae Mivart, 1865	*Cebus* Erxleben, 1777 *Saimiri* Voigt, 1831
	Atelinae Miller, 1924	*Ateles* Geofory, 1806 *Brachyteles* Spix, 1823 *Lagothrix* Geoffory, 1812
	Callimiconinae Thomas, 1913	*Callimico* Ribeiro, 1911
Callithricidae Thomas, 1903		*Callithrix* Erxleben, 1777 *Leontocebus* Wagner, 1839
Cercopithecidae Gray, 1821	Cercopithecinae Blanford, 1888	*Macaca* Lacepede, 1799 *Cynopithecus* Geoffroy, 1835 *Cercocebus* Geoffory, 1835 *Papio* Erxleben, 1777 *Comopithecus* Allen, 1925 *Mandrillus* Ritgen, 1824 *Theropithecus* Geofory, 1843 *Cercopithecus* Brunnich, 1772 *Allenopithecus* Lang, 1923 *Erythrocebus* Trouessart, 1897
	Colobinae Elliot, 1913	*Presbytis* Eschscholtz, 1821 *Pygathrix* Geoffroy, 1812 *Rhinopithecus* Milne Edwards, 1872 *Simias* Miller, 1903 *Nasalis* Geoffroy, 1812 *Colobus* Illiger, 1811
Pongidae Elliot, 1913	Hylobatinae Gill, 1872	*Hylobates* Illiger, 1811 *Symphalangus* Gloger, 1841
	Ponginae Allen, 1925	*Pongo* Lacepede, 1799 *Pan* Oken, 1816 *Gorilla* Geoffroy, 1852
Hominidae Gray, 1825		*Homo* Linnaeus, 1758

Used by permission of the American Museum of Natural History, New York, NY.

TABLE 1.7 COMMONLY USED CLASSIFICATION OF THE LIVING REPRESENTATIVES OF THE ORDER PRIMATES

FAMILY	GENERA
Cheirogaleidae	*Allocebus* *Cheirogaleus* *Microcebus* *Phaner*
Lemuridae	*Hapalemur* *Lemur* *Lepilemur* *Varecia*
Indriidae	*Indri* *Lichanotus* *Propithecus*
Daubentoniidae	*Daubentonia*
Lorisidae	*Arctocebus* *Loris* *Nycticebus* *Perodicticus*
Galagidae	*Galago* *Otolemur*
Tarsiidae	*Tarsius*
Callithricidae	*Callithrix* *Cebuella* *Leontopithecus* *Saguinus*
Callimiconidae	*Callimico*
Cebidae	*Alouatta* *Aotus* *Ateles* *Brachyteles* *Cacajao* *Callicebus* *Cebus* *Chiropotes* *Lagothrix* *Pithecia* *Saimiri*
Cercopithecidae	*Allenopithecus* *Cercocebus* *Cercopithecus* *Colobus* *Erythrocebus* *Macaca* *Nasalis* *Papio* *Presbytis* *Pygathrix* *Theropithecus*
Hylobatidae	*Hylobates*
Pongidae	*Gorilla* *Pan* *Pongo*
Hominidae	*Homo*

This classification was published by the American Society of Mammalogists in their synthesis of mammal taxonomy (Honacki, Kinman, and Koeppl, 1982) and has been widely employed in the literature.

1.32 Left lateral view of the snout region in a mounted aye-aye. The hairless rhinarium acts as a tactile organ, as do the obvious specialized tactile hairs (*vibrissae*). Lemurs have well-developed vibrissae but they are reduced in lorises and even

Vibrissae act as tactile organs, as does the rhinarium

Incisors are specialized in the aye-aye

more reduced or inconspicuous in monkeys and apes (Schultz, 1969). Vibrissae are considered to be part of the ancestral primate morphotype.

Specimen courtesy of Yale Peabody Museum

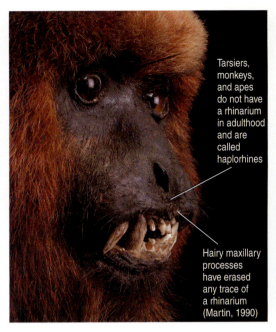

Tarsiers, monkeys, and apes do not have a rhinarium in adulthood and are called haplorhines

Hairy maxillary processes have erased any trace of a rhinarium (Martin, 1990)

1.33 Tarsiers, New and Old World monkeys, apes, and humans are united as *haplorhines*. Haplorhine primates do not have a rhinarium and this permits greater mobility of the upper lip and therefore facial expression than in the strepsirhines.

Specimen courtesy of Yale Peabody Museum

the possession of a dental comb, a grooming claw on the second digit of their feet, postorbital bar rather than postorbital septum, a relatively small brain, a primitive nasal region with an ethmoid recess, tapetum lucidum in the eye, at least two pairs of nipples, a bicornuate uterus (two separate uterine horns), and epitheliochorial placentation (Fleagle, 1988). In contrast, haplorhines have postorbital septa (at least partial in tarsiers), a single chamber in the uterus (except tarsiers), haemochorial placentation, and a fovea in the temporal region of the retina. They lack a stapedial artery (branch of the internal carotid artery) in the intrabullar circulation, an ethmoidal recess in the nasal region, the rhinarium, and tapetum lucidum (Fleagle, 1988). Further contrasts between strepsirhines and haplorhines are discussed in Martin (1990). Groves (2001) enumerates the features that had led authors to classify tarsiers with strepsirhines as "prosimians": vertical clinging locomotor behavior, tarsal elongation, toilet claws, a short simple gut,

large olfactory bulbs, cerebellum visible in dorsal view, a large postorbital fissure, persistent metopic suture in the frontal region of the skull, and tribosphenic molars.

Platyrrhines Compared to Catarrhines

Groves (2001) divides the Haplorhini into the Tarsiiformes and Simiiformes at the level of the infraorder. At the next lower taxonomic level, the Simiiformes are divided into the Platyrrhini (New World monkeys) and Catarrhini (Old World monkeys, apes, and humans). The nostrils are widely separated in platyrrhines, generally rounded in shape and face laterally. Platyrrhines are also characterized by the possession of three premolars in each side of a jaw, an ear region that has the

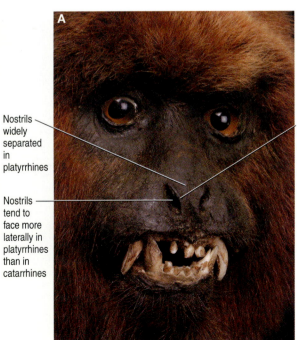

A

Nostrils widely separated in platyrrhines

Nostrils tend to face more laterally in platyrrhines than in catarrhines

Platyrrhiny is plesiomorphic (Maier, 2000)

B

Nares close together and oriented more downward or anteriorly than in platyrrhines

Nasal openings closer together in catarrhines than in platyrrhines because of narrowing of the medial lamella of the cupular cartilage (Maier, 2000)

1.34 A Mounted howler monkey (*Alouatta*). **B** Adult female Golden langur (*Trachypithecus [Presbytis] geei*). Comparison of the area of the nostrils to illustrate the differences in the platyrrhine and catarrhine conditions.

Specimen A courtesy of Yale Peabody Museum

Photo B courtesy of Dr. Thomas T. Struhsaker

tympanic ring fused to the auditory bulla but does not form a bony tube, lack of hypoconulids on the first two molars, and a pterion region "where the parietal and zygomatic bones join to separate the frontal bone above from the sphenoid below" (Fleagle, 1988:116). In catarrhines, the nasal openings are generally closer together than in platyrrhines, are narrow and face more downward. Catarrhines have two premolars in each side of a jaw, a tubular external auditory meatus, and "the frontal bone contacts the sphenoid bone and separates the zygomatic bone anteriorly from the parietal bone posteriorly" (Fleagle, 1988:159) (Figure 1.35). There are also differences in the postcranial skeleton.

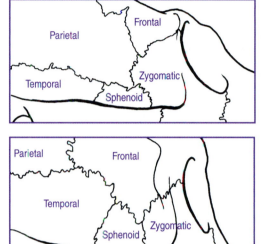

1.35 Drawings of the skull bone sutures in a mantled howler monkey (a) and a common chimpanzee (b). Note that the parietal and zygomatic bones articulate in the New World monkey (platyrrhine) to separate the frontal from the sphenoid. In catarrhines, including the chimpanzee, the frontal articulates with the sphenoid and separates the zygomatic and parietal bones. Note that the cranial landmark pterion is formed by the zygomatic and parietal bones in the New World monkey but by the frontal and temporal in the chimpanzee.

TABLE 1.8A RECENT CLASSIFICATION OF PRIMATES TO THE FAMILY LEVEL

SUBORDER	INFRAORDER	INTERMEDIATE LEVEL BETWEEN INFRAORDER AND SUPERFAMILY	SUPERFAMILY	FAMILY
Strepsirrhini	Lemuriformes		Cheirogaleoidea	Cheirogaleidae
			Lemuroidea	Lemuridae Megaladapidae Indridae
	Chiromyiformes			Daubentoniidae
	Loriformes			Loridae Galagonidae
Haplorrhini	Tarsiiformes			Tarsiidae
	Simiiformes	Platyrrhini		Cebidae Aotidae Pithecidae Atelidae
		Catarrhini	Cercopithecoidea	Cercopithecidae
			Hominoidea	Hominidae
				Hylobatidae

Source: *Primate Taxonomy* by Colin Groves, Smithsonian Institute, 2001.

TABLE 1.8B FAMILIES, GENERA AND COMMON NAMES OF PRIMATES IN GROVES (2001) CLASSIFICATION

FAMILY	GENERA	COMMON NAMES	FAMILY	GENERA	COMMON NAMES
Cheirogaleidae	Cheirogaleus	Dwarf lemurs		Callicebus	Titis
	Microcebus	Mouse-lemurs	Atelidae	Alouatta	Howler monkey
	Mirza	Giant mouse-lemur		Ateles	Spider monkeys
	Allocebus	Hairy-eared mouse-lemur		Brachyteles	Woolly spider monkeys
	Phaner	Fork-crowned lemurs		Lagothrix	Woolly monkeys
Lemuridae	Lemur	Ring-tailed lemur		Oreonax	Yellow-tailed woolly monkey
	Eulemur	Lemurs, including Brown, Black, Mongoose, etc.	Cercopithecidae	Allenopithecus	Swamp monkey
	Hapalemur	Gentle (Bamboo) lemurs		Miopithecus	Talapoin
	Varecia	Ruffed lemurs		Erythrocebus	Patas monkey
Megaladapidae	Lepilemur	Sportive lemurs, weasel lemur		[Chlorocebus][1]	Vervet monkey
				Cercopithecus	Guenons
Indridae	Indri	Indri		Macaca	Macaques
	Avahi	Avahis or woolly indris		Lophocebus	Gray-cheeked mangabey, crested mangabey, Opdenbosch's mangabey
	Propithecus	Sifaka		Papio	Baboons or savannah baboons
Daubentoniidae	Daubentonia	Aye-aye		Theropithecus	Gelada baboon
Loridae	Arctocebus	Angwatibos		Cercocebus	Sooty mangabey, Tana River mangabey, etc.
	Perodicticus	Potto		Mandrillus	Mandrills and drills
	Loris	Slender loris		Colobus	Black-and-white colobus, including black, angola, King, mantled, etc.
	Nycticebus	Slow loris			
Galagonidae	Otolemur	Greater galagos or thick-tailed bushbabies		Piliocolobus	Red colobus monkey
	Euoticus	Needle-clawed bushbabies		Procolobus	Olive colobus
	Galago	Bushbabies, including Lesser, Senegal, Prince Demidoff's, etc.		Semnopithecus	Gray langurs
				Trachypithecus	Lutungs or leaf-monkeys, langurs such as purple-faced, Nilgri, capped, etc.
Tarsiidae	Tarsius	Tarsiers			
Cebidae	Callithrix (includes pygmy marmoset)	Marmosets		Presbytis	Surilis, langurs such as white-fronted, Thomas's and Hose's, maroon leaf monkey
	Leontopithecus	Lion tamarins			
	Saguinus	Tamarins	Hylobatidae	Hylobates	Gibbon, siamang
	Callimico	Goeldi's marmoset	Hominidae	Pongo	Orangutan
	Cebus	Capuchin monkeys		Gorilla	Gorilla
	Saimiri	Squirrel monkeys		Pan	Common chimpanzee, pygmy chimpanzee
Nyctipithecidae	Aotus	Night monkeys			
Pithecidae	Pithecia	Saki monkeys		Homo	Humans
	Chiropotes	Bearded sakis			
	Cacajao	Uakaris			

[1] Genus name applied by Groves (2001) to African green monkeys (vervets, grivets) is in brackets because it is not accepted by Paul F. Whitehead. I have the utmost respect for Dr. Groves's experience but I believe that the characters that he uses to erect a separate genus are too subject to individual variation to be useful and that there is not sufficient difference in the adaptive strategies of vervet monkeys to separate them from the other Cercopithecus monkeys at the generic level.

Note: Groves (2001) is used as the taxonomic framework for presentation of material of extant species in subsequent chapters of the atlas, although alternative taxonomic terms (principally from Honacki, Kinman, and Koeppl, 1982) are presented wherever possible.

Body Organization

2

INTRODUCTION

Physical anthropology, also termed biological anthropology, is the study of human and non-human primate evolution, anatomy, physiology, and genetics. Other branches of anthropology focus on the study of culture. Physical anthropologists are interested in: 1) reconstructing the fossil history of primates, especially humans, 2) understanding the evolutionary relationships among living primates, 3) elucidating the functional significance of the features of primates, and 4) studying the social and maintenance behaviors of primates. The field formulates its own terminology and employs concepts and nomenclature from fields such as anatomy, genetics, paleontology, taphonomy, ecology, evolutionary biology, systematics, ethology, kinesiology, biomechanics, and statistics.

This chapter will not attempt to cover all of the terms found in the literature but will introduce some fundamental terms that will be useful in the undergraduate physical anthropology laboratory. This chapter will also briefly present some aspects of neural and muscular anatomy that are not covered in later chapters.

Whenever a physical anthropologist describes features of human anatomy, it is assumed that the discussion refers to the body in *anatomical position*. Anatomical position is the standardized reference position used to describe the location of anatomical parts. The body is erect and facing the observer, the arms are held at the sides, and the palms are also facing the observer. For example, the skeleton in Figure 2.1 is in anatomical position. Schultz (1969, Plate 7) basically places an adult male orangutan, chimpanzee, gorilla, and human in anatomical position although the feet are more abducted than is normal in anatomical position; in this standardized position, it is easy to compare body proportions in the four species. Unfortunately, anatomical position is not one that is naturally assumed by most pronograde primates because many are not able to supinate their forearms to the degree that is possible in humans.

THE HUMAN SKELETON

DIRECTIONAL TERMINOLOGY APPLIED TO THE HUMAN SKELETON

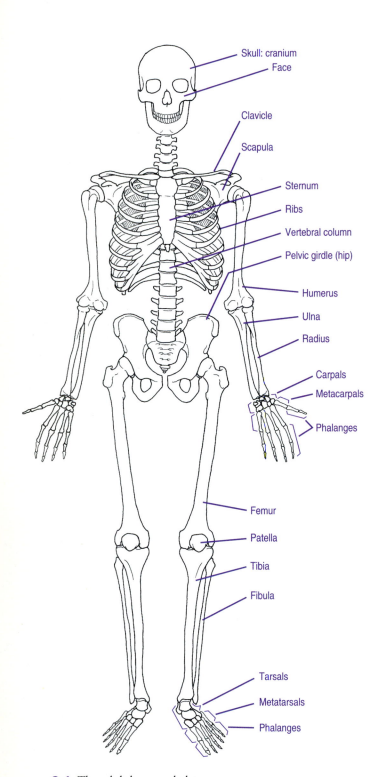

Skull: cranium
Face
Clavicle
Scapula
Sternum
Ribs
Vertebral column
Pelvic girdle (hip)
Humerus
Ulna
Radius
Carpals
Metacarpals
Phalanges
Femur
Patella
Tibia
Fibula
Tarsals
Metatarsals
Phalanges

2.1 The adult human skeleton.

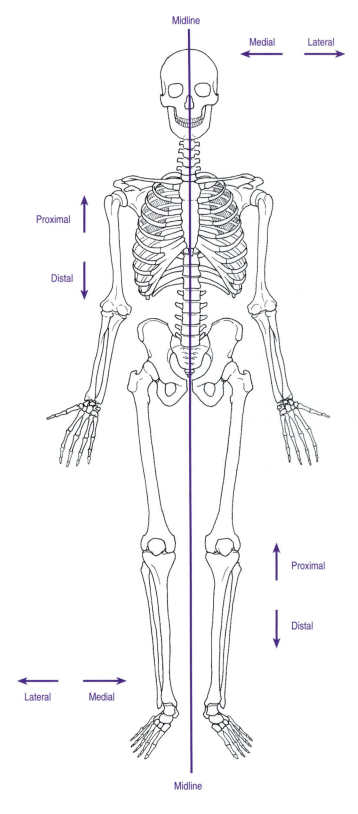

Midline
Medial   Lateral
Proximal
Distal
Proximal
Distal
Lateral   Medial
Midline

2.2 *Directional terms* are used to describe exactly where a structure is located. The terms are used for both bones and soft tissue structures.

TABLE 2.1 DIRECTIONAL TERMS APPLIED TO THE BODY, INCLUDING THE SKELETON

TERM	DEFINITION
Cranial, superior	Toward the head.
Caudal, inferior	Away from the head, toward the tail.
Ventral, anterior	Toward the belly.
Dorsal, posterior	Toward the back.
Medial	Toward or at the midline of the body.
Lateral	Away from the midline of the body.
Intermediate	Between two structures.
Proximal	Closer to the point of attachment of a limb to the trunk.
Distal	Farther from the point of attachment of a limb to the trunk.
Superficial	Toward or at the body surface.
Deep	Away from the body surface; more internal.

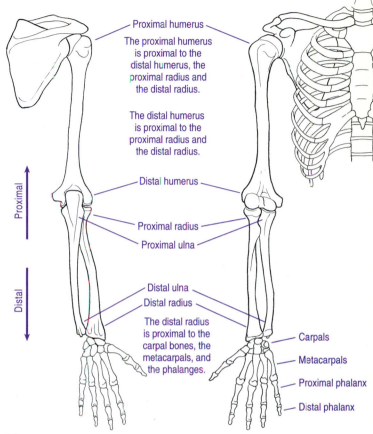

2.3 Directional terms applied to structures in the upper extremity (forelimb). The posterior aspect of the right upper extremity is on the left and the anterior aspect is on the right.

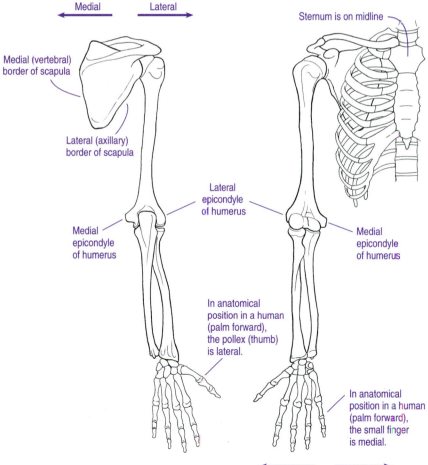

2.4 Directional terms applied to structures in the upper extremity (forelimb). The posterior aspect of the right upper extremity is on the left and the anterior aspect is on the right.

DIRECTIONAL TERMINOLOGY APPLIED TO THE DENTITION

TABLE 2.2 DIRECTIONAL TERMS AND SURFACES IN THE DENTITION	
TERM	**DEFINITION**
Distal	The surface of a tooth that faces along the dental arcade away from the midline.
Mesial	The surface of the tooth that faces along the dental arcade toward the midline.
Buccal	The surface of a canine, premolar or molar that faces the cheek.
Labial	The surface of an incisor that faces the lips.
Lingual	The surface of a tooth that faces the tongue.
Occlusal	The surface of a tooth that parallels the plane in which upper and lower dentitions meet. It is often used to describe the surfaces of upper and lower premolars and molars that meet during occlusion.
Incisal	The cutting edge of an incisor or canine.
Apical	The surface of a tooth that faces toward the apex of the root(s).

From *Dental Anthropology* by Simon Hillson, Table 2.2, page 12. Copyright © 1996. Reprinted with the permission of Cambridge University Press.

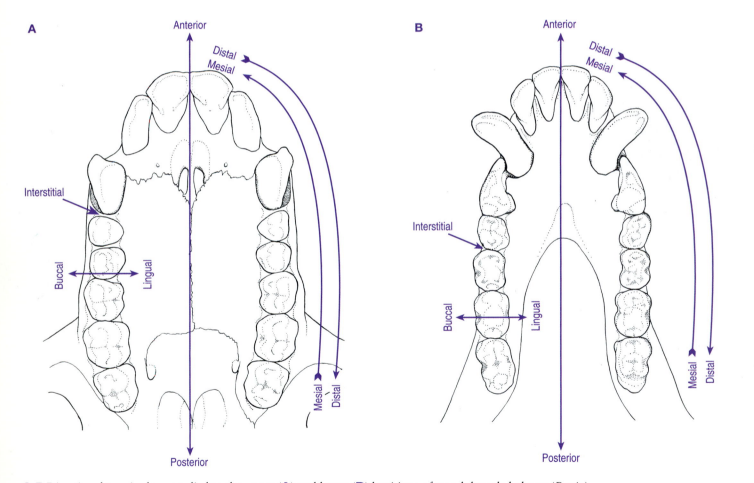

2.5 Directional terminology applied to the upper (**A**) and lower (**B**)dentitions of an adult male baboon (*Papio*).

PLANES OF THE BODY

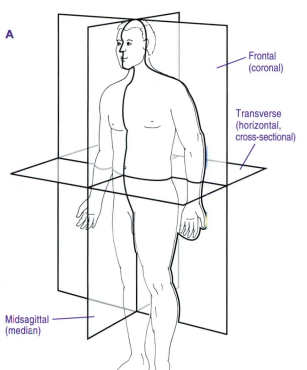

A

Frontal (coronal)

Transverse (horizontal, cross-sectional)

Midsagittal (median)

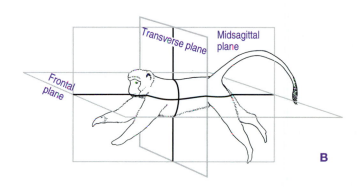

Transverse plane

Midsagittal plane

Frontal plane

B

2.6 A Planes of the body in a bipedal human and **B** a quadrupedal vervet monkey. Planes are imaginary flat surfaces that pass through the body and are used to describe the relationship in position among anatomical structures.

BODY CAVITIES

TABLE 2.3 BODY CAVITIES		
CAVITY	**DIVISIONS**	**DESCRIPTION**
Dorsal	Cranial	Houses brain and cranial meninges.
	Vertebral	Houses spinal cord and spinal meninges.
Ventral	Thoracic	
	Pleural	Encloses lung.
	Pericardia	Encloses heart.
	Abdominopelvic	
	Abdominal	Encloses stomach, small intestine, liver, etc.
	Pelvic	Encloses rectum, reproductive organs, bladder.
Oral, buccal		Mouth
Nasal	2 nasal fossae separated by nasal septum	Initial portion of conducting passages of respiratory system.
Paranasal sinuses		Four sets: one in each maxilla, one in sphenoid, one in ethmoid, one in frontal.
Orbital		Encloses eyeballs.
Middle ear (tympanic cavity)		Air-filled space within petrous portion of temporal bone; contains incus, malleus, stapes.
Inner ear		Contains cochlea, responsible for transduction and signal analysis.
Synovial		Enclosed within joint capsules of synovial joints.

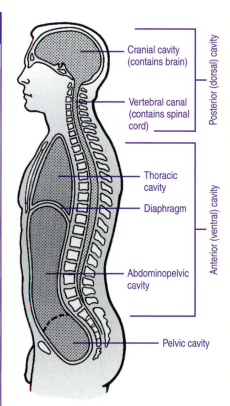

Cranial cavity (contains brain)

Vertebral canal (contains spinal cord)

Posterior (dorsal) cavity

Thoracic cavity

Diaphragm

Abdominopelvic cavity

Anterior (ventral) cavity

Pelvic cavity

2.7 Body cavities are spaces that contain internal organs.

HOMOLOGOUS BONES OF NONHUMAN PRIMATES

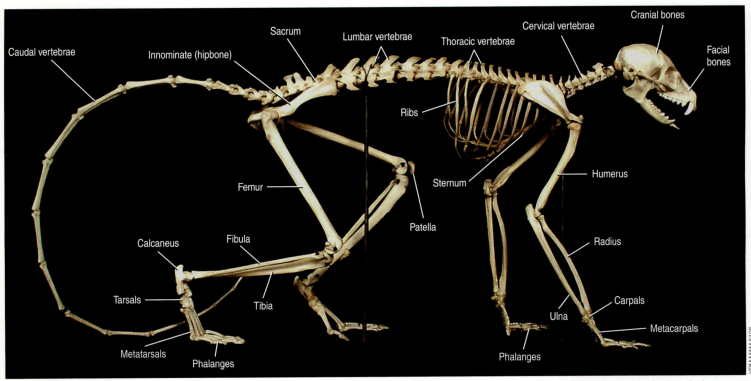

2.8 *Lemur catta.*

Specimen courtesy of Yale Peabody Museum

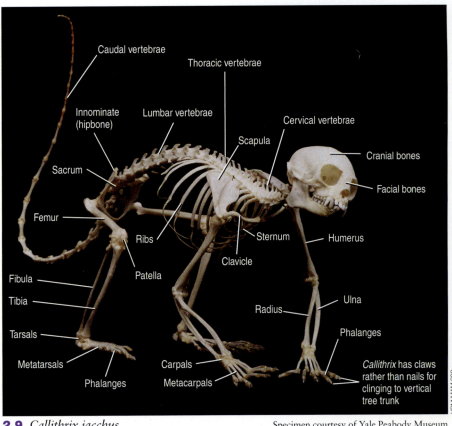

Callithrix has claws rather than nails for clinging to vertical tree trunk

2.9 *Callithrix jacchus.*

Specimen courtesy of Yale Peabody Museum

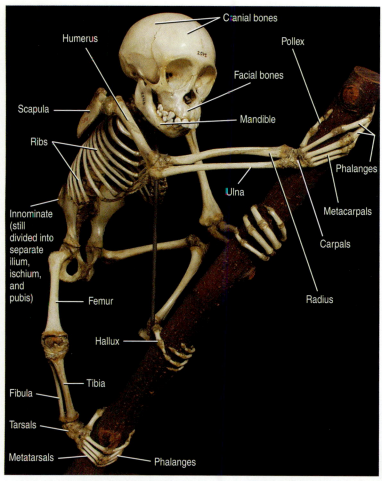

YPM MAM 2545

2.10 Immature *Pan troglodytes*.

Specimen courtesy of Yale Peabody Museum

MAJOR JOINTS OF THE PRIMATE SKELETON

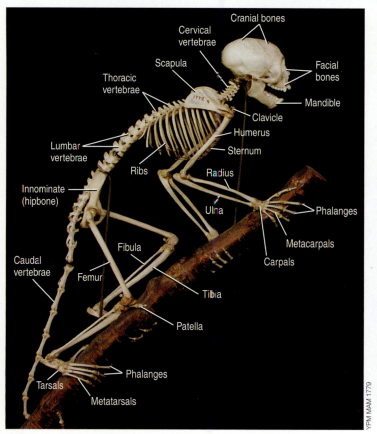

YPM MAM 1779

2.11 *Cebus capucinus.*

Specimen courtesy of Yale Peabody Museum

YPM MAM 1779

2.12 Major joints depicted in a skeleton of *Cebus capucinus*.

Specimen courtesy of Yale Peabody Museum

INTRODUCTION TO THE SUPERFICIAL MUSCLES OF THE HUMAN BODY

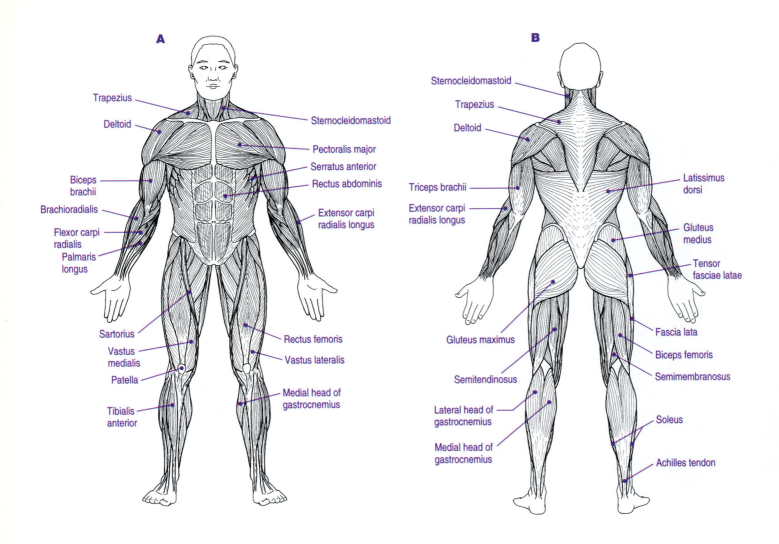

A

Trapezius

Deltoid

Biceps brachii

Brachioradialis

Flexor carpi radialis

Palmaris longus

Sartorius

Vastus medialis

Patella

Tibialis anterior

Sternocleidomastoid

Pectoralis major

Serratus anterior

Rectus abdominis

Extensor carpi radialis longus

Rectus femoris

Vastus lateralis

Medial head of gastrocnemius

B

Sternocleidomastoid

Trapezius

Deltoid

Triceps brachii

Extensor carpi radialis longus

Gluteus maximus

Semitendinosus

Lateral head of gastrocnemius

Medial head of gastrocnemius

Latissimus dorsi

Gluteus medius

Tensor fasciae latae

Fascia lata

Biceps femoris

Semimembranosus

Soleus

Achilles tendon

2.13 Superficial muscles. **A** Anterior view. **B** Posterior view. **C** Hindlimbs, left lateral view.

Visualizing Muscles: A New Approach to Surface Anatomy, by John Cody, M.D., © 1990 by the University Press of Kansas

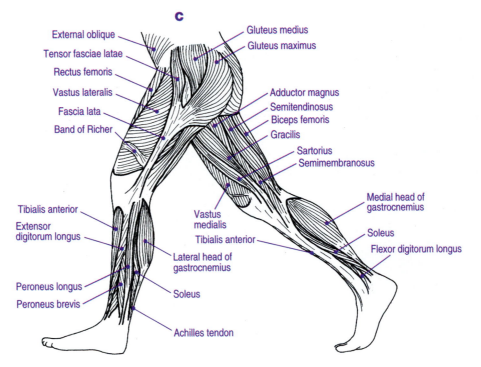

C

External oblique

Tensor fasciae latae

Rectus femoris

Vastus lateralis

Fascia lata

Band of Richer

Tibialis anterior

Extensor digitorum longus

Peroneus longus

Peroneus brevis

Gluteus medius

Gluteus maximus

Adductor magnus

Semitendinosus

Biceps femoris

Gracilis

Sartorius

Semimembranosus

Vastus medialis

Tibialis anterior

Lateral head of gastrocnemius

Soleus

Medial head of gastrocnemius

Soleus

Flexor digitorum longus

Achilles tendon

TABLE 2.4 TERMINOLOGY FOR SKELETAL MUSCLE

TERM	DEFINITION	EXAMPLE IN HUMANS
Agonist (mover, prime mover)	Muscle that is directly responsible for effecting a movement.	Masseter is prime mover of jaw closure.
Antagonist	A muscle that causes the opposite movement from that of the movers.	Triceps brachii is antagonist of forearm (elbow) flexors such as biceps brachii.
Aponeurosis	A fibrous sheet of connective tissue that attaches muscle to bone.	Internal oblique attaches to ventral midline from tenth costal cartilage to body of pubis via an aponeurosis.
Bipennate	Muscle fibers oblique to line of pull and attach to both sides of central septum and to its continuous central tendon.	Rectus femoris.
Direct or fleshy attachment (origin or insertion)	Epimysium of muscle is fused to periosteum of bone or perichondrium of cartilage.	Origin of temporalis.
Fascicle	Discrete bundle of muscle cells surrounded by a perimysium.	All skeletal muscles are composed of fasciculi., e.g., deltoid.
Indirect attachment (origin or insertion)	More common than direct attachment. Muscle fascia extends beyond muscle as a ropelike tendon or an aponeurosis.	Insertion of temporalis.
Insertion	End of the muscle that attaches to the bone that normally moves when the muscle contracts.	Insertions of masseter are the angle and ramus of the mandible.
Multipennate	Muscle fibers oblique to line of pull. In muscles that have several intermediate septa, each of which has a bipennate arrangement of fibers around it.	Deltoid.
Origin	End of the muscle that is on the bone that normally does not move when the muscle contracts.	Origins of masseter are the zygomatic arch and maxilla.
Parallel	Long axes of fascicles run with long axis of muscle.	Straplike: Sartorius Fusiform (expanded belly): Biceps brachii
Synergist	Muscle that cooperates in muscle functioning.	Medial pterygoid is synergist of temporalis and masseter in elevation of the lower jaw.
Neutralizer	Acts to prevent an undesired action of one of the movers.	Together, trapezius and rhomboids adduct the scapula without rotating it.
Stabilizer	Steadies or fixes the bone to which the contracting muscle is attached.	Scapular adductors and downward rotators prevent teres major from rotating scapula as it adducts humerus.
Unipennate	Muscle fibers oblique to line of pull and attach to one side of tendon only.	Extensor digitorum longus.

TABLE 2.5 ACTIONS OF SKELETAL MUSCLES

ACTION	DEFINITION	EXAMPLE IN HUMANS
Extension	Increase of angle between two bones in the paramedian plane.	Triceps brachii extends forearm (elbow).
Flexion	Decrease of angle between two bones in the paramedian.	Biceps brachii flexes elbow.
Hyperextension	Continuation of extension beyond the starting position or beyond the straight line.	Forearm is hyperextended if angle at elbow joint has exceeded 180 degrees.
Hyperflexion	When the arm is flexed beyond the vertical.	Refers to movement of the upper arm; in other joints, hyperflexion is prevented by contact of moving segment with another part of the body.
Lateral flexion (bending)	Movement, in the coronal plane, of the trunk (vertebral column) to one side.	Longissimus thoracis and cervicis bend the vertebral column laterally when they act on one side of the body.
Abduction	Movement, in the coronal plane, away from the midline of the body; in the case of fingers, away from the midline of the hand.	Deltoid abducts arm when all of its fibers contract simultaneously.
Adduction	Movement, in the coronal plane, toward the midline of the body.	Latissimus dorsi adducts arm.
Inversion	To orient the soles of the feet toward each other.	Tibialis posterior inverts foot.
Eversion	To orient the soles of the feet away from each other.	Peroneus longus everts foot.
Dorsiflexion (=flexion of the ankle)	At the ankle, to move the top of the foot toward the shin.	Tibialis anterior dorsiflexes foot.
Plantarflexion (=extension of the ankle)	At the ankle, to move the sole of the foot downward, as in standing on tiptoe.	Gastrocnemius plantarflexes foot when the knee is extended.
Elevation	Upward or superior movement.	Masseter elevates the mandible.
Depression	Downward or inferior movement.	Hyoglossus depresses the tongue.
Supination	To turn palm up or anterior.	Supinator supinates forearm.
Pronation	To turn palm down or posterior.	Pronator teres pronates forearm.
Rotation	Turning about the longitudinal axis of the bone.	
Medial	Toward midline of body ("inward").	Levator scapulae, rhomboids, latissimus dorsi, assisted by pectoral muscles, medially rotate scapula.
Lateral	Away from midline of body ("outward").	Trapezius and serratus anterior laterally rotate scapula.
Circumduction	A combination of movements in the sagittal and frontal planes, and in the oblique planes between them, which results in encompassing a cone. It is a combination of flexion, extension, adduction and abduction.	Motion of the hand at the wrist involving activity of flexors and extensors.

MIDSAGITTAL SECTION OF THE HUMAN HEAD (MRI)

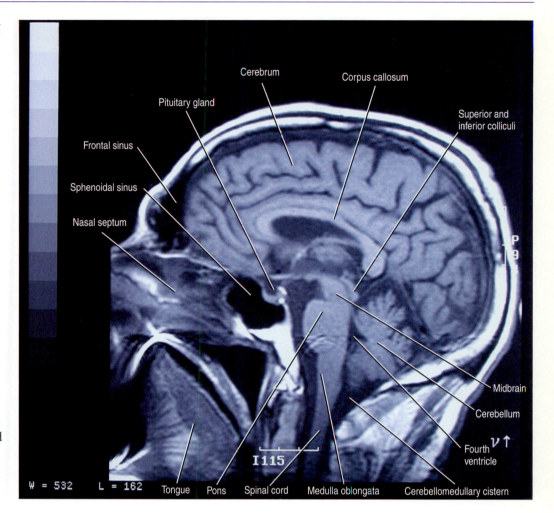

Cerebrum

Corpus callosum

Pituitary gland

Superior and inferior colliculi

Frontal sinus

Sphenoidal sinus

Nasal septum

Midbrain

Cerebellum

Fourth ventricle

Tongue   Pons   Spinal cord   Medulla oblongata   Cerebellomedullary cistern

W = 532   L = 162

I 115

2.14 Section depicts some major structures of the head in a modern human male subject, including some of the major structures of the brain.

TABLE 2.6 MAJOR FUNCTIONAL AREAS OF THE HUMAN BRAIN		
MAJOR AREA	**SOME MAJOR DIVISIONS[1]**	**FUNCTION**
Cerebrum	Frontal Lobe	
	Prefrontal area	Intellectual functions and personality.
	Premotor cortex	Skilled movements.
	Motor cortex	Voluntary movements.
	Broca's area	Control of the muscles that produce the sounds of speech.
	Parietal Lobe	
	Primary Somatosensory area	Cutaneous and muscular sensations (e.g., touch, pain).
	Occipital Lobe	
	Visual cortex	Vision.
	Temporal Lobe	
	Auditory cortex	Hearing.
	Olfactory cortex	Smell.
	Wernicke's area	Language.

Continued

[1] A complete anatomical and functional description of the brain is outside of the scope of this atlas. For further detail, please refer to Haines (1997), Kandel, Schwartz and Jessell (1991) or other references on the nervous system.

TABLE 2.6 MAJOR FUNCTIONAL AREAS OF THE HUMAN BRAIN *(continued)*

MAJOR AREA	SOME MAJOR DIVISIONS[1]	FUNCTION
Cerebellum	Arbor vitae, cerebellar peduncles, hemispheres, vermis	Body balance and position, coordinated movement
Pons	Pontine nuclei	Control breathing, 4 nuclei associated with cranial nerves
Medulla oblongata	Medial lemniscus, olive, pyramids.	Control and coordination centers for respiration and cardiovascular activity; centers for swallowing, vomiting, and cough reflexes; nuclei for five cranial nerves
Hypothalamus	Infundibulum, mammillary region, preoptic region, tuberal region, supraoptic region	Control area for autonomic nervous system, including control of body temperature, fluid balance, hunger, and control of pituitary gland
Thalamus	Intermediate mass, internal capsule, internal medullary lamina, 7 major groups of thalamic nuclei	Relay center for sensory nerve impulses except for smell
Basal nuclei (Ganglia)	Caudate nucleus, globus pallidus, putamen	Coordination and control of body movement; contribute to cognition
Reticular activating system	Network of neurons in brain stem, including medulla, pons and midbrain	Arousal, awareness
Limbic System	Cingulate gyrus, parahippocampal gyrus, hippocampus, dentate gyrus, amygdala, septal nuclei, mammillary bodies of hypothalamus, anterior and medial nuclei of thalamus, olfactory bulbs, fornix, stria terminalis, stria medullaris, medial forebrain bundle, mammillothalamic tract	Emotions

Reprinted from *Pathophysiology for the Health-Related Professions* by Barbara Gould, Table 20-2, page 324. Copyright © 1997, with permission from Elsevier.

CHAPTER THREE

Paleoanthropology | 3

Direct evidence for the evolutionary relationship of man and apes can only be supplied by paleontological studies, that is, by the discovery and examination of fossil remains of past ages.

Sir Wilfred E. Le Gros Clark (1967)
Man-Apes or Ape-Men? The Story of Discoveries in Africa

INTRODUCTION

Eugene Dubois had not yet discovered fossil human material in Java when Darwin wrote *The Descent of Man* and the significance of the Neandertal material had not been fully realized. The challenge was, at that time, to find the fossil evidence for human evolution. "For, if on the basis of indirect evidence intermediate phases of development from a common ancestral stock are postulated, then in the course of excavations in geological deposits relics of these phases might be expected to come to light in the search for fossils of extinct types" (Clark, 1967:5).

Despite the success that paleoanthropologists have had in unearthing the fossil and archeological record, the study of primate evolution remains one of the most contentious areas of evolutionary biology. There are a number of reasons for the debate.

Whenever a fossil is discovered, it must immediately be placed in a chronological framework. Unfortunately, this is not always as effortless as it may first appear. *Radiometric* dating methods, such as radiocarbon, potassium-argon and argon-argon have yielded important information. If a fossil is found *below* a basalt, for example, then we know that the fossil is older than the date obtained from that rock. Radiometric methods have permitted reliable dates to be obtained for some important sedimentary sequences that contain primate fossils, as in the case of Olduvai Gorge. However, if the fossil is *above* the dated rock, then we cannot give a precise estimate of the age of the remains. In addition, some major fossil sites (such as the South African australopithecine cave breccias and the locality TM 266 in Chad) do not have rocks that can be dated by current radiometric methods and so the paleoanthropologist must then rely on the less precise method of *faunal dating*. The

researcher compares the animal species found in the sediments to those found in other areas where radiometric dating was accomplished and then estimates a date for the sediments that cannot be dated directly by extrapolation. Sites that are dated faunally are frequently controversial in their placement in the chronology of human evolution.

Controversy also results from the incompleteness of the fossil remains. Even when a relatively complete specimen is found, subsequent additional material can revise ideas concerning the phylogenetic affinities and functional morphology of the specimen. This is particularly true when the initial find is fragmentary—a piece of mandible or maxilla, for example.

Researchers with different methodologies or conceptual frameworks also reach different conclusions about the same fossil. This is a particular concern in the study of the phylogenetic affinities and taxonomy of the fossil forms, and it can lead to confusing changes in systematic terminology. We briefly approached this issue in Chapter 1 when we presented some alternative taxonomies of the primates. An excellent example is the recent change, advocated by many paleoanthropologists, in the concept of *hominid*. For several decades, the term *hominid* had a very specific meaning—modern humans and their undoubted direct ancestors. The paradigm was a direct result of the "traditional" view that great apes and humans belonged to the same Superfamily Hominoidea, but were separated at the level of the Family into the Pongidae (chimpanzee, gorilla, and orangutan) and the Hominidae (humans and their direct ancestors). This was the framework in which paleoanthropologists couched their discussions until very recently. In the past few years, as a result of the dominance of cladistic systematics, there has been a movement to include the gorilla and chimpanzee within the Hominidae and to separate them from humans at the level of the subfamily. Modern humans and their direct ancestors are then assigned to the subfamily Homininae and are referred to as *hominins*.

At a lower taxonomic level, some paleoanthropologists have returned to a previously discarded terminology in discussions of the australopithecines. During the early studies of the australopithecines, fossils from Taung, Makapan and Sterkfontein had been placed in the genus *Australopithecus* and those from Kromdraai and Swartkrans had been distinguished by placement in a genus called *Paranthropus*. Washburn and Patterson (1951) advocated that the two forms actually were different species of the same genus. This viewpoint received widespread support, and the "gracile" and "robust" australopithecines were considered different species of *Australopithecus*. The grouping of the gracile and robust forms reached its extreme in the "Single-species Hypothesis," which argued that the two forms actually represented sexual dimorphism and should be placed in a single species (Brace, 1972). In recent years, some researchers (e.g., Tattersall and Schwartz, 2000) have reinstated *Paranthropus* for the robust forms but others (e.g., White, 2002) still place them within *Australopithecus*.

PALEOCENE FORMS
Plesiadapis fodinatus Jepsen, 1930a
Geological Age: Late Paleocene

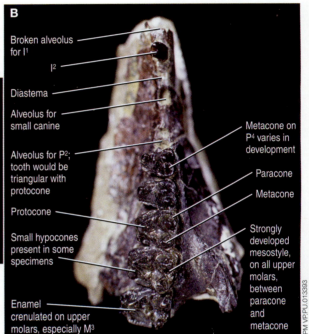

Broken alveolus for I[1]
I[2]
Diastema
Alveolus for small canine
Alveolus for P[2]; tooth would be triangular with protocone
Protocone
Small hypocones present in some specimens
Enamel crenulated on upper molars, especially M[3]
Metacone on P[4] varies in development
Paracone
Metacone
Strongly developed mesostyle, on all upper molars, between paracone and metacone

YPM VPPU.013393

3.1 Left maxilla of *Plesiadapis fodinatus* with I[2], P[3–4] and all upper molars. **A** Buccal aspect. **B** Occlusal aspect. Specimen is from the Polecat Bench Formation, Park County, Wyoming. It is dated to the Late Tiffanian. Gingerich (1976) describes the upper and lower dentition. The upper dental formula is 2.1.3.3. It is unfortunate that that the specimen does not preserve the central incisors because they have a characteristic morphology with well-developed anterocone, laterocone, and posterocone and a small mediocone. The lateral upper incisor is a small, caniniform tooth. The upper canine is actually smaller than I[2]. P[2] is described as small and narrow with a distolingual cingulum. P[3] is normally without a paraconule and the metacone varies in development. The metacone is consistently present on P[4] but the paraconule is sometimes lacking. The upper molars generally have a mesostyle. The enamel of the molars is usually crenulated, particularly on M[3].   *Specimen courtesy of Yale Peabody Museum*

A — Partial alveolus for I[1]
I[2] is curved, caniniform
Canine missing; Gingerich (1976) reports it is smaller than I[2] but similar in form
P[2] missing
P[3]
P[4]
M[1]
M[2]
M[2]

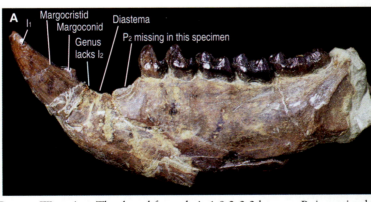

A — I[1]
Margocristid
Margoconid
Genus lacks I[2]
Diastema
P[2] missing in this specimen

3.2 Left side of the mandible of *P. fodinatus* with I, P[3–4], M[1–3].
A Buccal aspect.
B Occlusal aspect. It was collected in 1934 in the Late Tiffanian of Park County, Wyoming. The dental formula is 1.0.2-3.3 because P[2] is retained in several specimens. The lower incisor has a margoconid and margocristid. P[3–4] generally have basined "heels." M[1–2] possess curved, crested entoconids and M[3] has a broad, square, crenulated "heel" but lacks a distal cingulid.   *Specimen courtesy of Yale Peabody Museum*

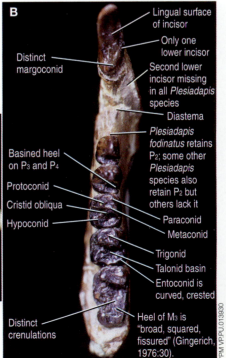

B — Lingual surface of incisor
Only one lower incisor
Second lower incisor missing in all *Plesiadapis* species
Diastema
Plesiadapis fodinatus retains P[2]; some other *Plesiadapis* species also retain P[2] but others lack it
Paraconid
Metaconid
Trigonid
Talonid basin
Entoconid is curved, crested
Heel of M[3] is "broad, squared, fissured" (Gingerich, 1976:30).
Distinct margoconid
Basined heel on P[3] and P[4]
Protoconid
Cristid obliqua
Hypoconid
Distinct crenulations

YPM VPPU.013930

Carpolestes dubius Jepsen, 1930b

YPM VP.PU.019422

3.3 *Carpolestes dubius.* **A** Occlusal aspect of the upper dentition. **B** Close-up of the upper cheekteeth. The specimen in Figure 3.3a is YPM VP.PU.019422. An accident at Yale shattered the right P³. Figure 3.3b is the right maxillary dentition of YPM VP.PU.014077 Both specimens are from the upper Polecat Bench Formation, Park County, Wyoming and are dated to the Late Tiffanian, late Paleocene. Note the polycuspate P³⁻⁴, a carpolestid trait. Jepsen (1930) and Rose (1975) describe the upper dentition. P³ has four well-developed buccal cusps. P² is a small, single-rooted tooth. P³

has three roots. There are three longitudinal rows of cusps on the latter tooth. P⁴ has an external row of five cusps and the enamel is crenulated. M¹ has a large protocone, well-developed paracone, metacone and hypocone. There are incipient developments of parastyle, mesostyle and metastyle on a cingulum. M² is basically similar, except for the development of mesostyle and hypostyle and less distinct ectocone.

Specimens courtesy of Yale Peabody Museum

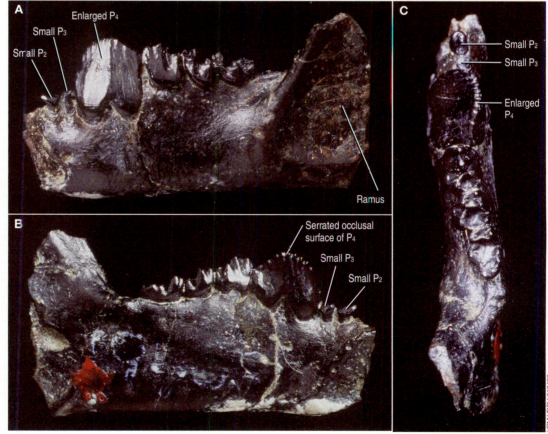

3.4 Lower dentition of *Carpolestes dubius.* **A** Buccal view. **B** Lingual view. **C** Occlusal view. Jepsen (1930) describes the lower dentition. The dental formula is ?1.0.4.3. P₂₋₃ are single-rooted. M₁ has two vertical ridges on the buccal side of a compressed, "trenchant" trigonid and three smaller serrations on the lingual side. M₁₋₂ have small but definite hypoconulids. Jepsen (1930) describes the M₃ as trilobate, with the mesial lobe having the protoconid and a higher, directly opposed cusp. He deduces that the paraconid and metaconid of M₃ form a single cusp. The marginal hypoconid is the largest cusp on the M₃. The entoconid is smaller than the hypoconid, is slightly distal and marginal. There are no diastemata between teeth.

Specimen courtesy of Yale Peabody Museum

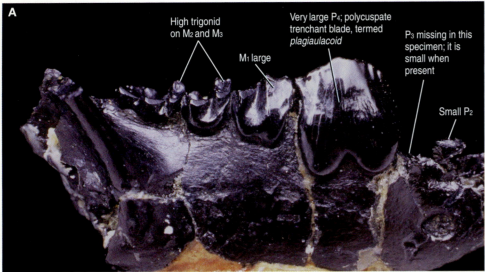

A

High trigonid
on M_2 and M_3

M_1 large

Very large P_4; polycuspate
trenchant blade, termed
plagiaulacoid

P_3 missing in this
specimen; it is
small when
present

Small P_2

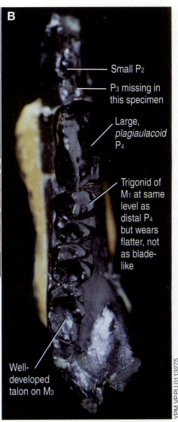

B

Small P_2

P_3 missing in
this specimen

Large,
plagiaulacoid
P_4

Trigonid of
M_1 at same
level as
distal P_4
but wears
flatter, not
as blade-
like

Well-
developed
talon on M_3

YPM VP.PU.0113275

3.5 Close-up of lower dentition of *C. dubius*. **A** Lateral view. **B** Occlusal view. The specimen is the holotype YPM VP.PU.013275, from the Polecat Bench Formation, Park County, Wyoming. It was collected by Glenn L. Jepsen and Joseph F. Page in 1929 and is dated to the late Tiffanian.   Specimen courtesy of Yale Peabody Museum

EOCENE PRIMATES

Adapiformes

(from Gebo, 2002 omitting Cercamoniinae, Sivaladapidae and problematic taxa, which are not figured in this atlas)

Order Primate Linnaeus, 1758
Suborder Strepsirhini É. Geoffroy Saint-Hilaire, 1812
   Infraorder Adapiformes Hoffstetter, 1977
     Family Notharctidae Trouessart, 1879
       Subfamily Notharctinae Trouessart, 1879
         Genera   *Cantius* Simons, 1962
              Copelemur Gingerich & Simons, 1977
              Hesperolemur Gunnell, 1995
              Notharctus Leidy, 1870
              Pelycodus Cope, 1875
              Smilodectes Wortman, 1903
     Family Adapidae Trouessart, 1879
       Subfamily Adapinae Trouessart, 1879
         Genera   *Adapis* Cuvier, 1821
              Adapoides Beard *et al*, 1994
              Cryptadapis Godinot, 1984
              Leptadapis Gervais, 1876
              Microadapis Szalay, 1974
              Palaeolemur Delfortrie, 1873

Tarsiiformes

(from Gunnell and Rose, 2002, but omitting problematic taxa and genera from tribes not figured in the atlas)

Order Primates Linnaeus, 1758
Suborder Prosimii Illiger, 1811 [Note that Groves would use Haplorhini which would be consistent with Strepsirhini used by Gebo, 2002]

Infraorder Tarsiiformes Gregory, 1915
   Family Omomyidae Trouessart, 1879
     Subfamily Microchoerinae Lydekker, 1887
       Genera   *Microchoerus* Wood, 1846
           Necrolemur Filhol, 1873
           Nannopithex Stehlin, 1916
           Pseudoloris Stehlin, 1916
     Subfamily Anaptomorphinae Cope, 1872
       Tribe Anaptomorphini
         Genera   *Anaptomorphus* Cope, 1872
            Tetonius Matthew, 1915
            Absarokius Matthew, 1915
            Teilhardina Simpson, 1940
            Anemorphysis Gazin, 1958
            Chlororhysis Gazin, 1958
            Pseudotetonius Bown, 1974
            Arapahovius Savage & Waters, 1978
            Aycrossia Bown, 1979
            Strigorhysis Bown, 1979
            Gazinius Bown, 1979
            Tatmanius Bown & Rose, 1991
     Subfamily Omomyinae Trouessart, 1879
       Tribe Omomyini
         Genera   *Omomys* Leidy, 1869
            Steinius Bown & Rose, 1984
            Chumashius Stock, 1933
       Tribe Rooneyini
         Genera   *Rooneyia* Wilson, 1966
       Tribe Macrotarsiini
         Genera   *Macrotarsius* Clark, 1941
            Hemiacodon Marsh, 1872
            Yaquius Mason, 1990

Teilhardina americana Bown, 1976
Geological Age: Early Eocene

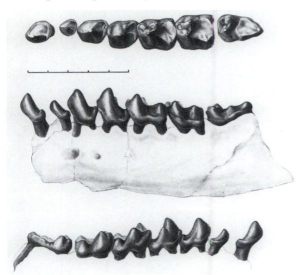

3.6 Lower left dentition of the holotype UW 6896 from Bown and Rose (1987:27). The specimen has its canine through M3. The species is an omomyid from the lower part of the Willwood Formation, early Wasatchian of Wyoming. The lower dental formula is 2.1.3-4.3 for the genus and it would be the only omomyid that retains P1. Bown and Rose (1987:27) considered *Teilhardina* to be "probably the basal omomyid . . . and is plausibly the common ancestor of all omomyids." The most diagnostic teeth are the P3–4. P3 is simple and unreduced, while P4 may have a small paraconid and metaconid and is not an enlarged tooth (Gunnell and Rose, 2002). *T. americana* possesses a slightly higher P4 metaconid than the type species *T. belgicus*. The lower cheekteeth are also relatively broader. The cheekteeth are also narrower than in *Teilhardina crassidens*, paraconid and metaconid are not present on P3, and P4 has a more open trigonid, weaker paraconid and lower and smaller metaconid than in *T. crassidens*.   Drawing by E. Kasmer, courtesy of Dr. Kenneth D. Rose

Tetonius matthewi Bown & Rose, 1987
Geological Age: Early Eocene

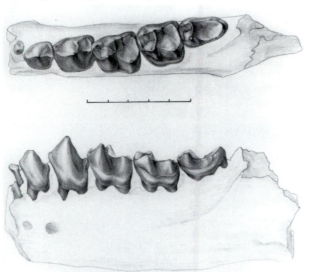

3.8 Left P2–M3 (YPM VP.023031). *T. matthewi* is described from the early Eocene of Wyoming and Colorado. It possesses a reduced P2, a relatively unreduced and double-rooted P3 and its anterior dentition is uncrowded. The figure is from Bown and Rose (1987:53).   Drawing by E. Kasmer, courtesy of Dr. Kenneth D. Rose

Comparison of Upper Cheekteeth in Species of *Teilhardina*
Geological Age: Early Eocene

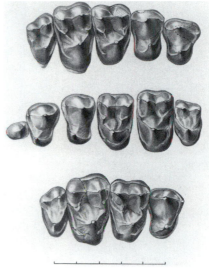

3.7 Comparison of upper cheekteeth in *T. crassidens* YPM VP.024626 right P3–M3 (top), *Teilhardina* intermediate UM 69783 left P2–M3 (middle), and *T. americana* UW 8871 right P4–M3 (bottom) from Bown and Rose (1987:30). The upper molars of *T. americana* show a "*Nannopithex*-fold."

Drawing by E. Kasmer, courtesy of Dr. Kenneth D. Rose

Pseudotetonius ambiguus Bown, 1974
Geological Age: Early Eocene

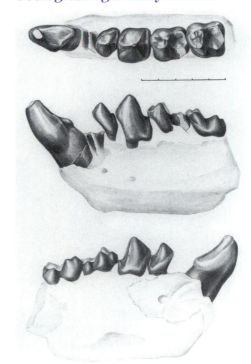

3.9 The species is from the Willwood Formation of Wyoming and the Wasatch Formation of Colorado. The figured specimen is from Bown and Rose (1987:62) and is MCZ 19010, left lower jaw with I1, P3–M2 and alveoli for the lateral lower incisor and canine. Top is occlusal, middle is lateral, and bottom is medial views. Bown and Rose (1987) diagnose *Pseudotetonius* as an anaptomorphine that was similar in size to *Tetonius* but with: a dental formula of 2.1.2.3, P3 reduced relative to P4, P3 with one mesiodistally compressed root, canine and second lower incisor smaller and more compressed, central lower incisor more robust, and antemolar portion of dentary is shorter.

Drawing by E. Kasmer, courtesy of Dr. Kenneth D. Rose

Absarokius abbotti Loomis, 1906

Geological Range: Early to early Middle Eocene in Wyoming; Late Early Eocene in Colorado

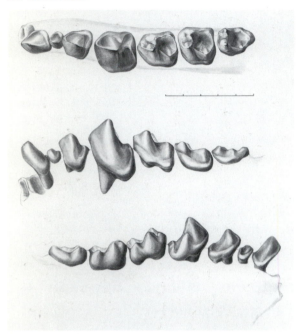

3.10 This is the type species for the genus *Absarokius*. Gunnell and Rose (2002) describe the dentition. The lower dental formula is 2.1.3.3 and the upper is 2.1.3.3. The P_4 is enlarged and buccally expanded. P^4 is enlarged, narrower and more quadrate than in *Pseudotetonius* and *Tetonius* and the third molars are relatively smaller. "*Absarokius* further differs from *Pseudotetonius* in having a much smaller I_1 and a larger C and differs from *Tetonius* in having I_{1-2} much smaller and P_2 much larger" (Gunnell and Rose, 2002). Bown and Rose (1987) detail morphological trends and regional variation in morphology between species, and highlight tendencies toward larger mean cheektooth size, hypertrophy of P_4, and progressive ventral enlargement of the distobuccal portion of P_4. The figured specimen is from Bown and Rose (1987:68): YPM VP.027791, left lower jaw with canine, P_3–M_3, and alveoli for lower central and lateral incisors. Top is occlusal, middle is lateral and bottom is medial view.

Drawing by E. Kasmer, courtesy of Dr. Kenneth D. Rose

Cantius trigonodus Matthew, 1915

Geological Range: Early to possibly Middle Eocene

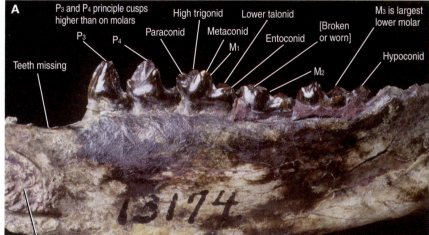

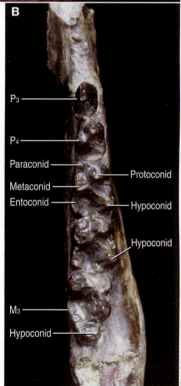

3.11 Right side of mandible with P_{3-4}, M_{1-3}. **A** Lingual aspect. **B** Occlusal aspect. The specimen is from the Willwood Formation, Big Horn County, Wyoming and was collected by L.L. Cook in 1928. Gebo (2002) describes notharctines, such as *Cantius*, as possessing: spatulate lower incisors with the central smaller than the lateral incisor, interlocking and sexually dimorphic canines, a honed premolar, and reduced or absent paraconids. Note the presence of four premolars. M_3 is long and has a long "heel." Unlike *Notharctus*, the mandibular symphysis is unfused. Szalay and Delson (1979) place this species in *Pelycodus*, but Gebo (2002) follows Simons (1962) in placing most species (with the exceptions of *P. danielsae* and *P. jarrovii*) in *Cantius*. Fleagle (1988) estimates the body weight to have been 2,000g in this species.

Specimen courtesy of Yale Peabody Museum

3.12 Anterior aspect of three femora of *Cantius abditus*. Fleagle (1988) estimates body weight to have been 3,000g in *C. abditus*.

Specimen courtesy of Yale Peabody Museum

Leptadapis magnus Filhol, 1874
Geological Range: Middle Eocene

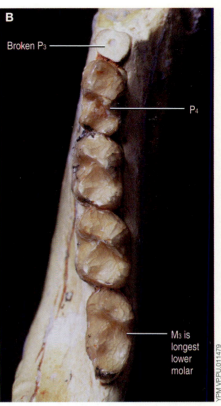

3.13 P4–M3 of the left side of the mandible. **A** Buccal aspect. **B** Occlusal aspect. The specimen is from the Headonian of the Midi-Pyrenees Region, France. The crown of P3 is broken. The dental formula is 2.1.4.3 (Szalay and Delson, 1979). This is the type species of the genus. *Leptadapis* is a European member of the subfamily Adapinae. Gebo (2002:30) states that the species was folivorous and that the "skulls show large sagittal crests and wide zygomatic regions associated with powerful chewing muscles . . ." which are typically more developed than in *A. parisiensis* (Simons, 1972). Unfortunately, the incisors and canine are not present in this specimen as they are different in morphology from those of *Adapis*, and the P2 (which is not present here) is reduced in size. Simons (1972) placed the species in *Adapis*.   Specimen courtesy of Yale Peabody Museum

Adapis parisiensis Cuvier, 1821
Geological Age: Late Eocene

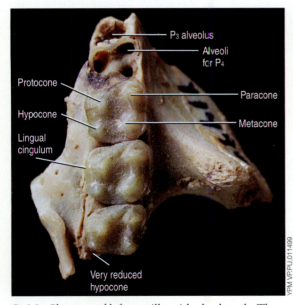

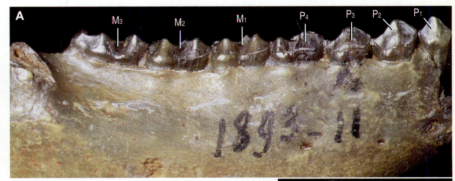

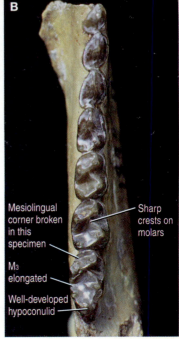

3.14 Close-up of left maxilla with cheekteeth. The specimen is from the upper Eocene phosphorites of Caylus, France. The P4 is more molariform than are the other upper premolars, with three major cusps— a condition that is different from that seen in modern lemurs. *Adapis* was the first genus of fossil primate to be described, with the initial discoveries made in quarry sites in the middle Eocene deposits of Montmartre, Paris (Simons, 1972). It is considered to belong to the same subfamily as *Leptadapis*: Adapinae.

Specimen courtesy of Yale Peabody Museum

3.15 Right side of the mandible of *A. parisiensis*. **A** Buccal aspect. **B** Occlusal aspect. P4 is also molariform. Note that the other premolars are narrow. There are shearing crests on the lower molars and it is believed that the species was folivorous.   Specimen courtesy of Yale Peabody Museum

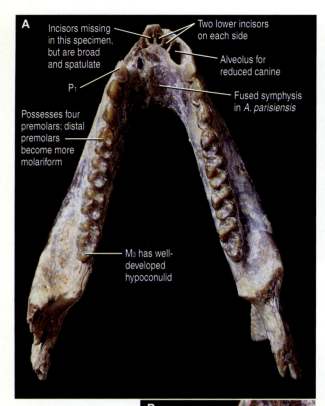

A — Incisors missing in this specimen, but are broad and spatulate

P₁

Two lower incisors on each side

Alveolus for reduced canine

Fused symphysis in *A. parisiensis*

Possesses four premolars; distal premolars become more molariform

M₃ has well-developed hypoconulid

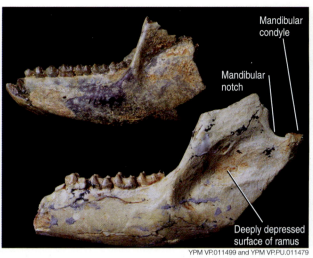

Mandibular condyle

Mandibular notch

Deeply depressed surface of ramus

YPM VP.011499 and YPM VP.PU.011479

3.17 Comparison of the size of *A. parisiensis* (upper) and *L. magnus* (lower). Fleagle (1988) estimates a body size of 1,300g for *A. parisiensis* and either 4,000g (p. 297) or 8.5kg (p. 299) for *L. magnus*.

Specimens courtesy of Yale Peabody Museum

3.16 A Occlusal aspect of the entire lower jaw. **B** Close-up of the cheekteeth on left side. Note that the mandibular symphysis is fused, unlike the condition seen in modern lemurs. It is unfortunate that the specimen lacks the anterior dentition because the lower incisors and canines form a single functional complex that may represent an incipient tooth comb.

Specimen courtesy of Yale Peabody Museum

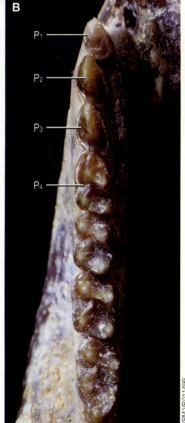

B

P₁

P₂

P₃

P₄

YPM VP.011499

Hemiacodon Marsh, 1872 or *Macrotarsius jepseni* Robinson, 1968
Geological Range: Late early and middle Eocene

A — Omomyines have relatively small lower central incisors that may be somewhat procumbent or vertically implanted

3.18 Left side of the mandible. **A** Buccal view. **B** Occlusal view. This specimen is identified in the Peabody Museum collections as *H. jepseni*, a species that is not recognized by Gunnell and Rose (2002), from the Uinta Formation, Uinta County, Utah. However, it is the holotype for *Macrotarsius jepseni*. *Hemiacodon* is an omomyine. There are sharply defined crests on all molars, a short but prominent talonid on P₄ with well-defined hypoconid and entoconid but no crista obliqua, P₄ has buccal and ligual ridges, hypoconulids on M₁₋₂ are sharp and arcuate, and rugose enamel on molar talonids—particularly evident on M₃ in this specimen (Gunnell and Rose, 2002). *Macrotarsius* is most closely related to *Hemiacodon* and can be separated from the other genus by: "P³ lingually broader with hypocone shelf better developed; upper molars with relatively weaker conules, moderate stylar shelves, and a well-developed mesostyle; upper molars more squared with lower, weaker hyocones and pericones; lower molar trigonids closed lingually and distally, and metaconid marginal and uninflated basally; and M₃ as broad as M₁₋₂."

Specimen courtesy of Yale Peabody Museum

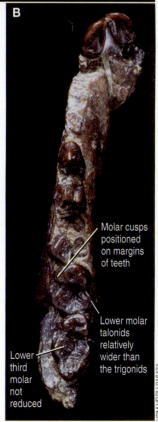

B

Molar cusps positioned on margins of teeth

Lower molar talonids relatively wider than the trigonids

Lower third molar not reduced

YPM VP.PU.016431

Necrolemur antiquus Filhol, 1873
Geological Range: Middle to Late Eocene

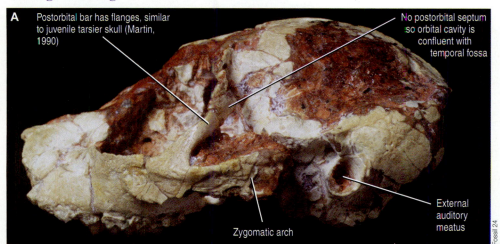

A Postorbital bar has flanges, similar to juvenile tarsier skull (Martin, 1990)

No postorbital septum so orbital cavity is confluent with temporal fossa

External auditory meatus

Zygomatic arch

Fossil 24

3.19 The genus is a member of the subfamily Microchoerinae of the Omomyidae. Skull of *Necrolemur*, a well-known omomyid from Europe. **A** Left lateral view. **B** Superior view. **C** Basicranial view. The inferior aspect of the auditory bulla had been dessicted by a previous researcher, but the view clearly shows that there was an inflated bulla with a tube-like auditory meatus. The superior view demonstrates the lack of a postorbital septum. It has large orbits and a relatively short snout. There are square upper molars with distinct hypocones, but the upper premolars are more triangular.

Specimens courtesy of Yale Peabody Museum

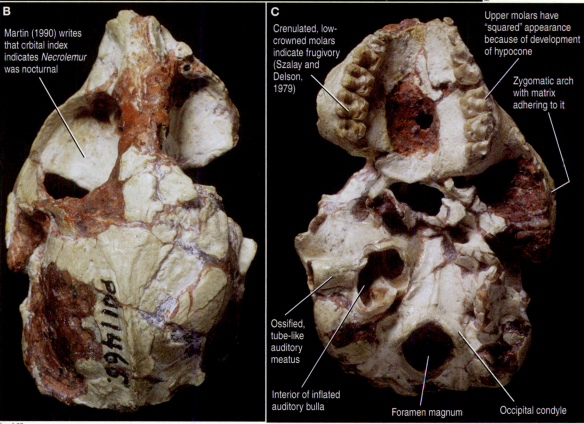

B Martin (1990) writes that orbital index indicates *Necrolemur* was nocturnal

Fossil 22

C Crenulated, low-crowned molars indicate frugivory (Szalay and Delson, 1979)

Upper molars have "squared" appearance because of development of hypocone

Zygomatic arch with matrix adhering to it

Ossified, tube-like auditory meatus

Interior of inflated auditory bulla

Foramen magnum

Occipital condyle

YPM VPPU.011465

B Bicuspid P4

Protoconid

Hypoconid

Small paraconid on M1

Metaconid

Entoconid

Paraconid lost in M2 and M3

M3 smaller than M2

Hypoconulid

Broken coronoid process

Mandibular condyle (condylar process)

YPM VPPU.011466

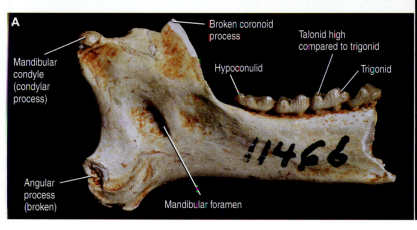

A

Broken coronoid process

Talonid high compared to trigonid

Hypoconulid

Trigonid

Mandibular condyle (condylar process)

Angular process (broken)

Mandibular foramen

3.20 Partial lower jaw. **A** Lingual aspect. **B** Occlusal aspect. The mandibular angle is described as short and broad (Gunnell and Rose, 2002). The M3 is reduced.

Specimen courtesy of Yale Peabody Museum

Notharctus tenebrosus Leidy, 1870
Geological Range: Middle to Late Eocene

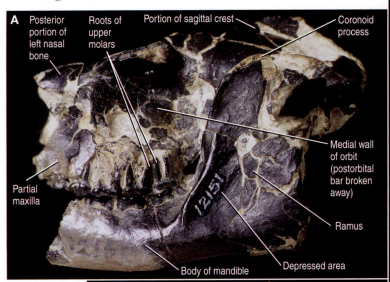

A
Posterior portion of left nasal bone

Roots of upper molars

Portion of sagittal crest

Coronoid process

Medial wall of orbit (postorbital bar broken away)

Ramus

Partial maxilla

Body of mandible

Depressed area

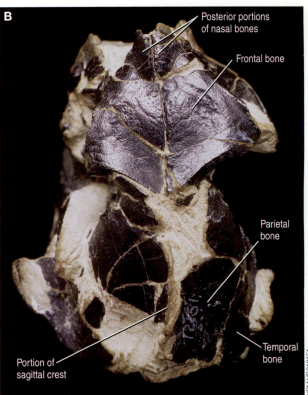

B
Posterior portions of nasal bones

Frontal bone

Parietal bone

Temporal bone

Portion of sagittal crest

3.21 Partial, crushed skull from the Bridger Formation, Wyoming. **A** Left lateral view. **B** Superior view. **C** Basicranial view. The genus is from late Wasatchian to Bridgerian sediments of North America. Fleagle estimates its body weight to have been 4,200g (p. 294). The face is longer than in the related *Smilodectes* and the orbits are relatively small, suggesting diurnal behavior.

Specimen courtesy of Yale Peabody Museum

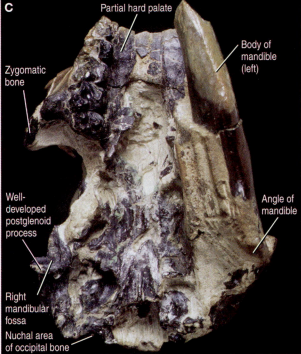

C
Partial hard palate

Body of mandible (left)

Zygomatic bone

Well-developed postglenoid process

Angle of mandible

Right mandibular fossa

Nuchal area of occipital bone

A
Plaster

Root of upper left canine

I¹ crown larger than I²

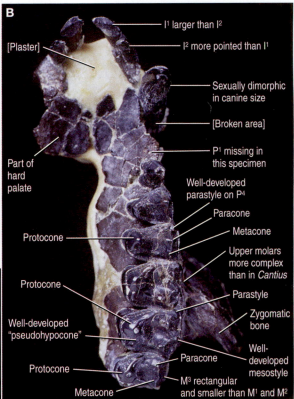

B
I¹ larger than I²

[Plaster]

I² more pointed than I¹

Sexually dimorphic in canine size

[Broken area]

P¹ missing in this specimen

Well-developed parastyle on P⁴

Paracone

Metacone

Upper molars more complex than in *Cantius*

Parastyle

Zygomatic bone

Well-developed mesostyle

Part of hard palate

Protocone

Protocone

Well-developed "pseudohypocone"

Protocone

Paracone

Metacone

M³ rectangular and smaller than M¹ and M²

3.22 Partial upper dentition from the Bridger Formation, Wyoming. **A** Left lateral aspect. **B** Occlusal aspect. White areas are reconstructed with plaster. There are larger pseudohypocones and mesostyles on the more complex upper molars than in *Cantius*, narrower upper molars, and a quadrate M³ (Gebo, 2002).

Specimen courtesy of Yale Peabody Museum

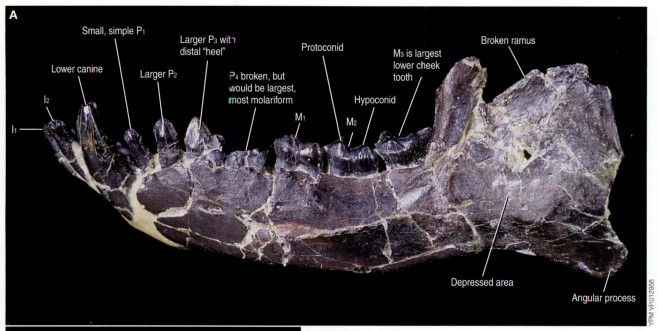

A

Lower canine

Small, simple P₁

Larger P₂

Larger P₃ with distal "heel"

P₄ broken, but would be largest, most molariform

Protoconid

Hypoconid

M₃ is largest lower cheek tooth

Broken ramus

I₁

I₂

M₁

M₂

Depressed area

Angular process

YPM VP:012956

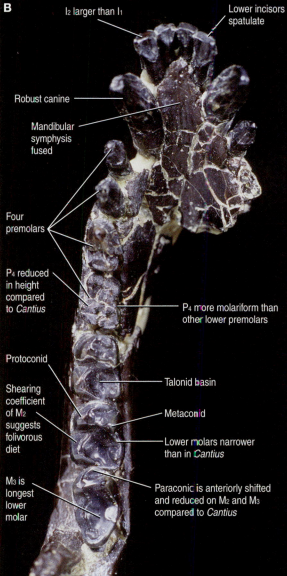

B

I₂ larger than I₁

Lower incisors spatulate

Robust canine

Mandibular symphysis fused

Four premolars

P₄ reduced in height compared to *Cantius*

Protoconid

Shearing coefficient of M₂ suggests folivorous diet

M₃ is longest lower molar

P₄ more molariform than other lower premolars

Talonid basin

Metaconid

Lower molars narrower than in *Cantius*

Paraconic is anteriorly shifted and reduced on M₂ and M₃ compared to *Cantius*

3.23 Partial mandible, preserving the entire left lower dentition but only I₁–P₁ on the right. **A** Buccal aspect. **B** Occlusal aspect. There are entoconid notches on P₄–M₃, a mesially shifted and reduced paraconid on M₂₋₃, and a shorter height for P₄ than in *Cantius* . It is suggested that the species was sexually dimorphic because of its canines. Shearing crests on the molars indicate a folivorous diet.

Specimen courtesy of
Yale Peabody Museum

3.24 Anterior aspect of a partial humerus of *Notharctus*. The humeral head faces posteriorly and is oval in outline. Note that the greater and lesser tuberosities are below the level the cranial surface of the humeral head, allowing more flexion at the shoulder than in a primate with high tuberosities. The deltopectoral crest extends further distally than in modern "prosimians." The genus is considered to have been arboreal in its behavior (Gebo, 1993b).

Specimen courtesy of
Yale Peabody Museum

Greater tuberosity

Humeral head is higher than both greater and lesser tuberosities

Lesser tubercle

Lesser tuberosity

Delto-pectoral crest

YPM VP:012956

YPM VP:012956

Rooneyia viejaensis Wilson, 1966
Geological Range: Latest Eocene

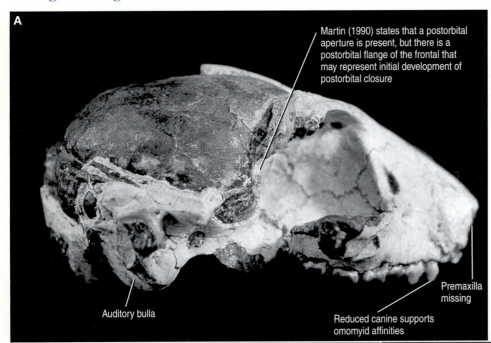

A

Martin (1990) states that a postorbital aperture is present, but there is a postorbital flange of the frontal that may represent initial development of postorbital closure

3.25 Skull TMM 40688-7. **A** Right lateral view. **B** Frontal view. **C** Basicranial view. The fossil was discovered in western Texas. *Rooneyia* had a postorbital aperture, but there is a postorbital flange of the frontal that may be interpreted as an incipient development of postorbital closure (Martin, 1990). The orbital index suggests diurnal habits. Note that there is a short bony auditory tube adjacent to the bulla.

Photographs courtesy of the Vertebrate Paleontology Laboratory, Texas Memorial Museum of Science and History, The University of Texas at Austin

Auditory bulla

Premaxilla missing

Reduced canine supports omomyid affinities

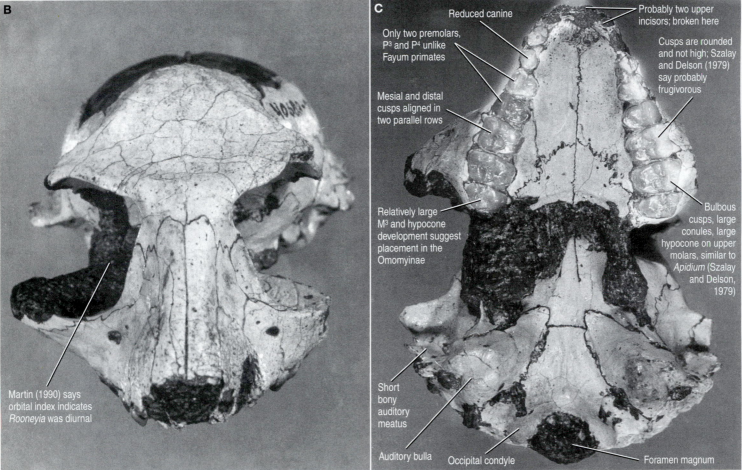

B

Martin (1990) says orbital index indicates *Rooneyia* was diurnal

C

Reduced canine

Only two premolars, P³ and P⁴ unlike Fayum primates

Mesial and distal cusps aligned in two parallel rows

Relatively large M³ and hypocone development suggest placement in the Omomyinae

Probably two upper incisors; broken here

Cusps are rounded and not high; Szalay and Delson (1979) say probably frugivorous

Bulbous cusps, large conules, large hypocone on upper molars, similar to *Apidium* (Szalay and Delson, 1979)

Short bony auditory meatus

Auditory bulla   Occipital condyle   Foramen magnum

"ANTHROPOID" PRIMATES

Eocene

Catopithecus browni Simons, 1989

Rasmussen (2002):

Order Primates Linnaeus, 1758
Infraorder Catarrhini É. Geoffroy Saint-Hilaire, 1812
　Superfamily Propliopithecoidea Simons, 1965
　　Family Oligopithecidae Kay & Williams, 1994
　　　Genus and Species: *Catopithecus browni* Simons, 1989

Geological Range: Late Eocene

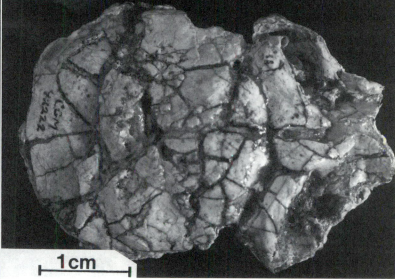

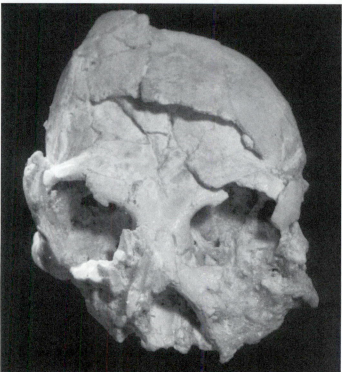

3.26 The skull (DPC 8701) was discovered at Locality 41 of the Fayum, Egypt. Simons (1989, 1990) describes the morphology. It is almost complete but is missing the anterior rostrum and suffered postmortem distortion. The skull is about the size of that of Goeldi's Marmoset. The frontal resembles that of *Apidium phiomense*. There is complete fusion of the frontal bone, the zygomatic bone indicates that there was a postorbital plate rather than postorbital bar (see Chapter 1), the orbit suggests diurnal habits, and the ectotympanic is in the lateral wall of the auditory bulla (as in *Aegyptopithecus*). Simons (1990) states that the specimen lacks an ectotympanic tube, so it is not similar to omomyids; it is also dissimilar to adapids because the ectotympanic does not form a free ring within the bulla. The mandibular fossa is described as broad, there is a postglenoid process and postglenoid foramen. The skull has P³–M³ and an alveolus for a small-to-medium-sized canine. The upper dental formula is interpreted as ?2-1-2-3, which is a catarrhine dental formula. The upper teeth show well-developed cingula, lack accessory upper molar cuspules (lack para-and metaconules), have hypocones on M¹⁻² and small mesostyle nodules on upper molars. Lower molars decrease in size distally and the mandibular symphysis was not fused. Simons (1990) concludes that *Catopithecus* was a primitive "anthropoidean," that manifests relationships to both adapids and propliopithecids.   Photographs Courtesy of Dr. Elwyn Simons, Duke University

Map of Some Major Oligocene and Miocene Fossil Sites

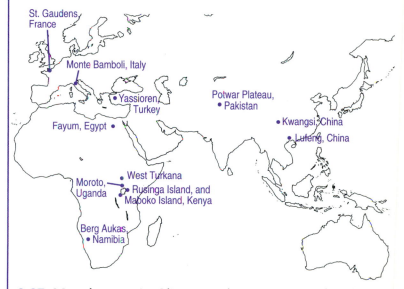

3.27 Map of some major Oligocene and Miocene primate fossil localities.

Oligocene

Apidium phiomense Osborn, 1908

Beard (2002):

Order Primates Linnaeus, 1758
Suborder Haplorhini Pocock, 1918
   Infraorder Anthropoidea Mivart, 1864
     Family Parapithecidae Schlosser, 1910
       Genus and Species: *Apidium phiomense* Osborn, 1908

Geological Range: Early Oligocene

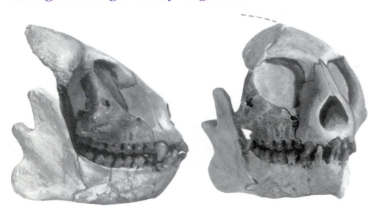

3.28   Right lateral (left) and right oblique (right) views of the reconstructed partial skull and occluded mandible. In January, 1967, Elwyn Simons found associated cranial and palatal fragments and upper teeth of *A. phiomense*. An important part of the discovery was a partial frontal bone with part of the interorbital septum. Simons (1972) describes the frontal as completely fused, unlike that found in lemurs. The mandibular symphysis is also fused. The dental formula is 2.1.3.3 upper and 2.1.3.3. lower. Beard (2002:143) believes that the olfactory bulbs were "relatively voluminous for an anthropoid of its size" and describes the zygomaticofacial foramen as large. Simons (1972) describes the upper teeth as mesiodistally short with separated cusps. Cheek teeth are bunodont, upper premolars have well-developed paraconules, and upper molars have lingual cingula, hypocones and pericones (Beard, 2002). Simons (1970, 1972) discussed "polycuspidation" and the presence of a lower molar "centroconid," as a result of which he suggested affinities to *Oreopithecus*. Later, he (1974) proposed that it had special affinities to Old World Monkeys. More recently, it has been suggested that parapithecids are the sister group of both catarrhines and platyrrhines (Fleagle and Kay, 1987).
Courtesy of Dr. Elwyn Simons, Duke University

3.30   Frontal view of two skulls (CGM 40237 and DPC 2803) unearthed since the original discovery in 1966. The new material demonstrates individual and age-related variability. Simons (1987) describes the specimens. They confirm that M^2 is the largest of the three upper molars. There are mesial grooves in the upper canines that terminate at the alveolar border. The lingual cingula have a "beaded" appearance. Simons (1987) favorably compares the dentition to *Afropithecus* and to *Proconsul*. The face has undoubtedly similarities to *Afropithecus*: the frontal bone and face are aligned, there is a broad interorbital septum, "bean-shaped" orbital outline, flaring lacrimals and a double transverse torus in the mandible. Simons (1987) particularly points to the depth of the combined maxilla and zygomatic below the orbit, the depth of the alveolar process of the maxilla, the broad interorbital septum, the presence of a sagittal crest, and anteromedial frontal ridges in discussing the robustness of the specimens.
Photo courtesy of Dr. Elwyn Simons, Duke University

Propliopithecus haeckeli Schlosser, 1910

Rasmussen (2002)

Order Primates Linnaeus, 1758
Infraorder Catarrhini
   Superfamily Propliopithecoidea Simons, 1965
     Family Propliopithecidae Straus, 1961
       Genus and Species *Propliopithecus haeckeli* Schlosser, 1910

Geological Age: Probably early Oliocene

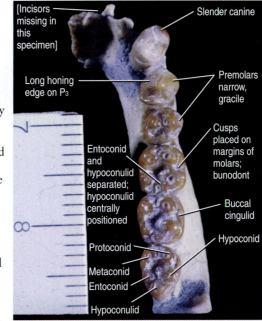

3.29   Occlusal view of the type female mandible SNM 12638, Stuttgart, with C–M₃. The type may be from Quarry G, Fayum, Egypt. The species is considered to be early Oligocene, from the lower part of the upper sequence of the Jebel, Qatrani Formation, Egypt. *P. haeckeli* is described as a small species with small, rounded premolars and thin canines (Rasmussen, 2002). It has bunodont molar cusps, central positioning of the hypoconulid, and lower molars that have marginally-placed cusps. Upper molars are square in shape with relatively large hypocones. There are buccal cingula on premolars and molars.   Courtesy of and copyright © Dr. Eric Delson

Aegyptopithecus zeuxis Simons, 1965

Rasmussen (2002):

Order Primates Linnaeus, 1758
Infraorder Catarrhini
   Superfamily Propliopithecoidea Simons, 1965
     Family Propliopithecidae Straus, 1961
       Genus and Species *Aegyptopithecus zeuxis* Simons, 1965

Geological Age: Upper sequence of the Jebel Qatrani Formation, early Oligocene

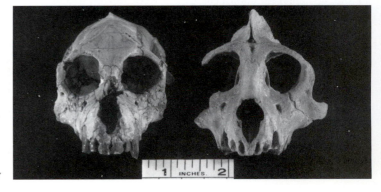

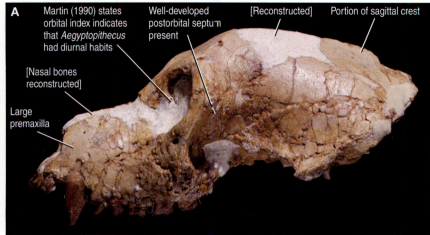

A

Martin (1990) states orbital index indicates that *Aegyptopithecus* had diurnal habits

[Nasal bones reconstructed]

Large premaxilla

Well-developed postorbital septum present

[Reconstructed]

Portion of sagittal crest

B

Distinct trigon

M² is largest upper molar

Condylar fossa

Occipital condyle

Protocone

Paracone

Protocone

Paracone

Metacone

Hypocone

Lingual cingulum

Well-developed postglenoid process

Martin (1990) states that ectotympanic ring is fused to outer margin of auditory bulla but not extended to form a bony tubular meatus

Foramen magnum

3.31 First *Aegyptopithecus* skull to be discovered, collected by Grant E. Meyer in 1966 in Quarry M, upper fossil wood zone, Jebel el Qatrani Formation, Fayum, Egypt. **A** Left lateral aspect. **B** Basicranial aspect. Note that a well-developed postorbital septum is present (see Chapter 1). There is a long, narrow snout with a large premaxilla. Rasmussen (2002) describes the interorbital distance as broad, with two plates of bone separating the orbits rather than one interorbital septum. The basicranial view demonstrates the bicuspid premolars, the large size of M², and the staggered arrangement of the principal cusps of M^{1-2}. The apex of the paracone is mesial to the apex of the protocone, and the apex of the metacone is mesial to the apex of the hypocone. There is a well-developed crista obliqua between the metacone and protocone. All three upper molars have lingual cingula. M² is markedly larger than is M¹ and it is also larger than M³. The four principal molar cusps are distinct on M^{1-2}. The ectotympanic ring is fused to the outer margin of the auditory bulla and does not form a tubular meatus. Conroy (1987) and Fleagle (1988) estimate body weight at 6–8kg. Rasmussen (2002) states that the frontal lobes of the cerebrum were smaller, and the olfactory bulbs were larger, than in any living "anthropoid".

Photos courtesy of William Sacco

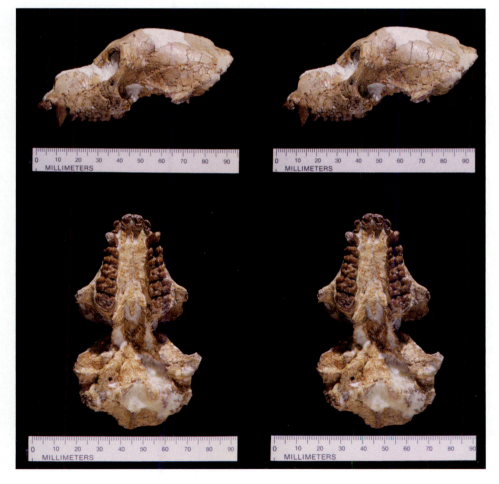

3.32 Stereograph views of the two aspects in Figure 3.31.

Courtesy of William Sacco

Miocene

REVISED ANCESTRAL CATARRHINE CRANIAL MORPHOTYPE

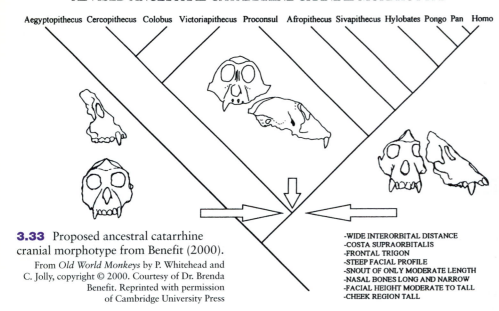

Aegyptopithecus Cercopithecus Colobus Victoriapithecus Proconsul Afropithecus Sivapithecus Hylobates Pongo Pan Homo

-WIDE INTERORBITAL DISTANCE
-COSTA SUPRAORBITALIS
-FRONTAL TRIGON
-STEEP FACIAL PROFILE
-SNOUT OF ONLY MODERATE LENGTH
-NASAL BONES LONG AND NARROW
-FACIAL HEIGHT MODERATE TO TALL
-CHEEK REGION TALL

3.33 Proposed ancestral catarrhine cranial morphotype from Benefit (2000).
From *Old World Monkeys* by P. Whitehead and C. Jolly, copyright © 2000. Courtesy of Dr. Brenda Benefit. Reprinted with permission of Cambridge University Press

3.34 Frontal (top) and left lateral (bottom) views of male cranium KNM-MB 29100 from the Maboko Formation, Kenya, dated to between 14.8-16 Ma. The Victoriapithecidae are an extinct family of Cercopithecoidea. They share a number of derived features with other Cercopithecoidea. Benefit (2000, Benefit and McCrossin, 2002) discusses their relationship to other ceropithecoids, the reconstruction of their diet and habits, the significance of their morphology for the reconstruction of the ancestral catarrhine cranial morphotype, and for the understanding of the cercopithecoid-hominoid split about 25 million years ago.
From *Old World Monkeys* by P. Whitehead and C. Jolly, copyright © 2000. Courtesy of Dr. Brenda Benefit. Reprinted with permission of Cambridge University Press

Victoriapithecus macinnesi von Koenigswald, 1969

Benefit and McCrossin (2002):

Order Primates Linnaeus, 1758
Infraorder Catarrhini É. Geoffroy Saint-Hilaire, 1812
　　Superfamily Cercopithecoidea Gray, 1821
　　　Family Victoriapithecidae von Koenigswald, 1969
　　　　Genus and Species *Victoriapithecus macinnesi* von Koenigswald, 1969

Geological range: 19-12.5 Ma

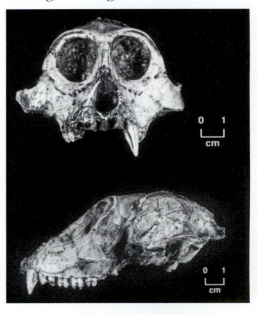

Turkanopithecus kalakoensis Leakey & Leakey, 1986

Harrison (2002):

Order Primates Linnaeus, 1758
Infraorder Catarrhini É. Geoffroy Saint-Hilaire, 1812
　Superfamily Proconsuloidea Leakey, 1963
　　Family Proconsulidae Leakey, 1963
　　　Subfamily Nyanzapithecinae Harrison, 2002
　　　　Genus and Species *Turkanopithecus kalakoensis* Leakey & Leakey, 1986

Geological range: 17.7-16.6 Ma

3.35 Right oblique view of the partial face and cranium described by Leakey and Leakey (1986a). The specimen is short-faced, with an additional cuspule on M² between the beaded mesial and lingual cingula, small additional cuspules associated with a small buccal cingulum bordering the paracone on P⁴ and the upper molars. These features distinguish the specimen from known hominoids. The palate is shallow and toothrows converge distally. The nasal aperture is high and narrow. The upper molars are wider than long. M²>M³>M¹. There is no supraorbital sulcus. The interorbital distance is large. There is a postglenoid process. The zygomatic process is relatively deep below the orbit.

Copyright © National Museums of Kenya

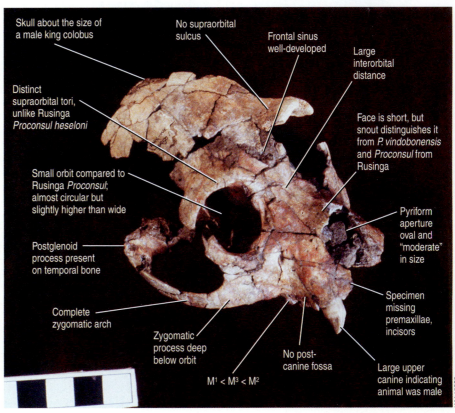

Skull about the size of a male king colobus

No supraorbital sulcus

Frontal sinus well-developed

Large interorbital distance

Distinct supraorbital tori, unlike Rusinga *Proconsul heseloni*

Face is short, but snout distinguishes it from *P. vindobonensis* and *Proconsul* from Rusinga

Small orbit compared to Rusinga *Proconsul*; almost circular but slightly higher than wide

Postglenoid process present on temporal bone

Pyriform aperture oval and "moderate" in size

Specimen missing premaxillae, incisors

Complete zygomatic arch

Zygomatic process deep below orbit

No post-canine fossa

M¹ < M³ < M²

Large upper canine indicating animal was male

WK 16950

Afropithecus turkanensis Leakey & Leakey, 1986

Harrison (2002):

Order Primates Linnaeus, 1758
Infraorder Catarrhini É. Geoffroy Saint-Hilaire, 1812
   Superfamily Proconsuloidea Leakey, 1963
     Family Proconsulidae Leakey, 1963
       Subfamily Afropithecinae Andrews, 1992
         Genus and Species *Afropithecus turkanensis*
         Leakey and Leakey, 1986

Geological Range: 17.7-17Ma

3.36 Type Specimen KNM-WK 16999 from Kalodirr, Kenya. **A** Frontal view. **B** Right lateral view. It is the face and partial cranium. Leakey and Walker (1997) state that the face is about the same size as that of a male *P. troglodytes* and estimate a body size of 34kg. They (1997:233) describe *Afropithecus* as a large hominoid that is "close to the condition of the stem catarrhine" in many characters but "highly derived in its feeding apparatus" with cusp morphology, lack of large shearing crests and large incisors that suggest frugivory but also thick enamel and heavy dental wear. They interpret the species as feeding on hard-shelled fruits (sclerocarp feeding). The overall facial proportions are similar to those of the smaller *Aegyptopithecus* (Fig. 3.30). Ward (1997) considers its facial proportions to be similar to those of *Sivapithecus*, although Leakey and Walker (1997:235) regard it to be too derived to belong to the same clade. In the original description, Leakey and Leakey (1986:143) describe it as a large species that is distinguished from other hominoids by a long muzzle and steeply inclined frontal "such that in lateral profile, prosthion, rhinion, glabella and bregma are on almost the same line . . ." This description was later echoed by Simons (1987) in his discussion of *Aegyptopithecus*. The palate is shallow, long, narrow and the tooth rows converge distally.

Copyright © National Museums of Kenya

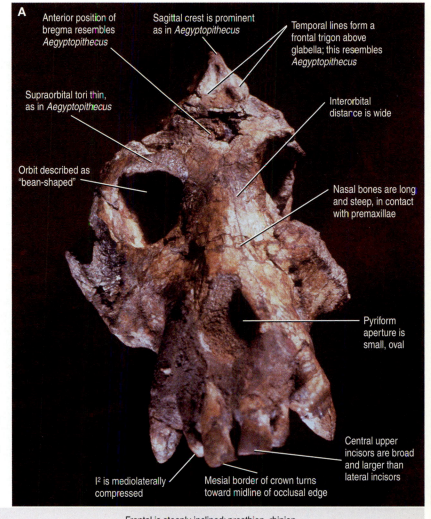

A
- Anterior position of bregma resembles *Aegyptopithecus*
- Sagittal crest is prominent as in *Aegyptopithecus*
- Temporal lines form a frontal trigon above glabella; this resembles *Aegyptopithecus*
- Supraorbital tori thin, as in *Aegyptopithecus*
- Interorbital distance is wide
- Orbit described as "bean-shaped"
- Nasal bones are long and steep, in contact with premaxillae
- Pyriform aperture is small, oval
- Central upper incisors are broad and larger than lateral incisors
- I^2 is mediolaterally compressed
- Mesial border of crown turns toward midline of occlusal edge

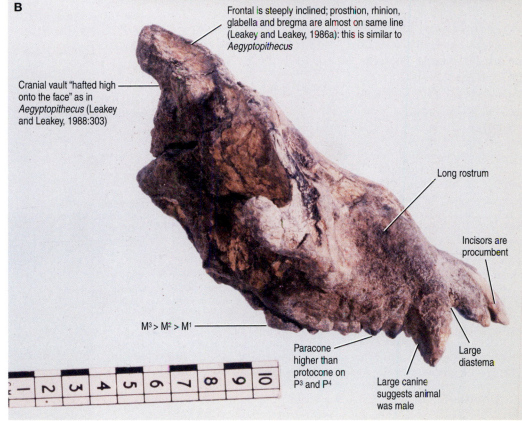

B
- Frontal is steeply inclined; prosthion, rhinion, glabella and bregma are almost on same line (Leakey and Leakey, 1986a): this is similar to *Aegyptopithecus*
- Cranial vault "hafted high onto the face" as in *Aegyptopithecus* (Leakey and Leakey, 1988:303)
- Long rostrum
- Incisors are procumbent
- Large diastema
- $M^3 > M^2 > M^1$
- Paracone higher than protocone on P^3 and P^4
- Large canine suggests animal was male

Morotopithecus bishopi Gebo et al, 1997

Harrison (2002):

Order Primates Linnaeus, 1758
Infraorder Catarrhini É. Geoffroy Saint-Hilaire, 1812
    Superfamily Hominoidea Gray, 1825
        Family *incertae sedis*
            Genus and Species *Morotopithecus bishopi* Gebo et al, 1997

Geological Age: 20.6 Ma or 15 Ma

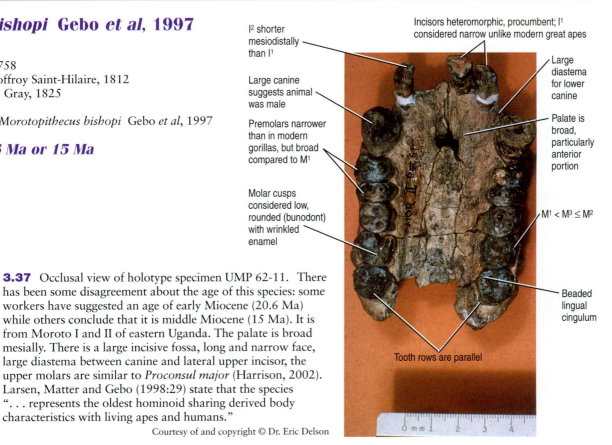

I² shorter mesiodistally than I¹

Incisors heteromorphic, procumbent; I¹ considered narrow unlike modern great apes

Large canine suggests animal was male

Large diastema for lower canine

Premolars narrower than in modern gorillas, but broad compared to M¹

Palate is broad, particularly anterior portion

Molar cusps considered low, rounded (bunodont) with wrinkled enamel

M¹ < M³ ≤ M²

Beaded lingual cingulum

Tooth rows are parallel

3.37 Occlusal view of holotype specimen UMP 62-11. There has been some disagreement about the age of this species: some workers have suggested an age of early Miocene (20.6 Ma) while others conclude that it is middle Miocene (15 Ma). It is from Moroto I and II of eastern Uganda. The palate is broad mesially. There is a large incisive fossa, long and narrow face, large diastema between canine and lateral upper incisor, the upper molars are similar to *Proconsul major* (Harrison, 2002). Larsen, Matter and Gebo (1998:29) state that the species ". . . represents the oldest hominoid sharing derived body characteristics with living apes and humans."

Courtesy of and copyright © Dr. Eric Delson

Dryopithecus fontani Lartet, 1856

Dryopithecus was first described in the mid-nineteenth century by Eduard Lartet from the site of Saint Gaudens, France. In the 1960's, all species of large Miocene ape were included in this genus. In recent years, workers have shifted back to considering *Dryopithecus* to be different from *Proconsul* and *Kenyapithecus*. The genus *Dryopithecus* is now used for European fossils from the middle to upper Miocene period, 13-9 Ma (Köhler, Moyà-Solà and Alba, 2001).

Begun (2002) and Kelley (2002):

Order Primates Linnaeus, 1758
Infraorder Catarrhini É. Geoffroy Saint-Hilaire, 1812
    Superfamily Hominoidea Gray, 1825
        Family Hominidae Gray, 1825
            Subfamily Homininae Gray, 1825
                Tribe Dryopithecini Gregory & Hellman, 1939
                    Genus and Species *Dryopithecus fontani* Lartet, 1856

Geological Range: 12-11 Ma

3.38 Occlusal view of the male mandible described by Albert Gaudry in 1890. The species is known from France and Austria. The male mandible decreases in height from the symphysis to the third lower molar. The male mandibles are among the largest in the genus *Dryopithecus*. Begun (2002) describes upper and lower dentitions: the incisors are robust, canines are compressed, premolars and molars are mesiodistally elongated. The molars do not possess cingula. The lower incisors are narrow and have high crowns. The lower canines are strongly compressed buccolingually. The Y-shaped pattern is present on the lower molars, and was referred to as the "Dryopithecus Y pattern" for many years.

Courtesy of and copyright © Dr. Eric Delson

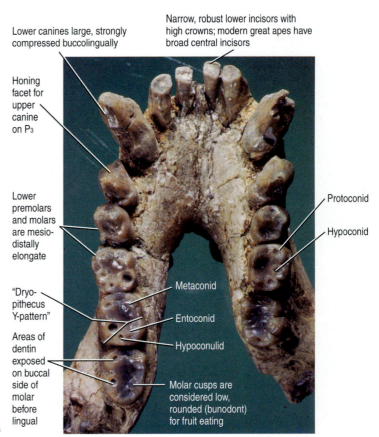

Lower canines large, strongly compressed buccolingually

Narrow, robust lower incisors with high crowns; modern great apes have broad central incisors

Honing facet for upper canine on P₃

Lower premolars and molars are mesio-distally elongate

"Dryo-pithecus Y-pattern"

Areas of dentin exposed on buccal side of molar before lingual

Metaconid

Entoconid

Hypoconulid

Molar cusps are considered low, rounded (bunodont) for fruit eating

Protoconid

Hypoconid

SIVAPITHECUS

Kelley (2002):

Order Primates Linnaeus, 1758

Infraorder Catarrhini É. Geoffroy Saint-Hilaire, 1812
  Superfamily Hominoidea Gray, 1825
    Family Hominidae Gray, 1825
      Subfamily Ponginae Elliot, 1913
        Tribe Sivapthecini
          Genus *Sivapithecus* Pilgrim, 1910

Sivapithecus indicus Pilgrim, 1910

Geological Range: 12.5–10.5 Ma

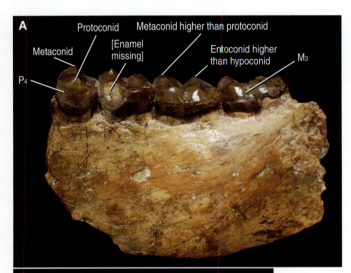

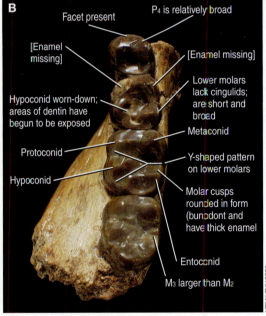

3.39 YPM.VP.013828 collected by N.K.N. Aiyengar, Yale-Cambridge (North) India Expedition of 1935 at Hari Talyangar, Bilaspur Kehloor State, India. **A** Lateral aspect. **B** Occlusal aspect. It is a partial lower jaw with P₄–M₃ from the Nagri Formation, which Simons and Pilbeam (1978) estimated spanned from about 7 Ma to about 10 Ma in age based on included fauna. Simons and Pilbeam (1965) referred it to *Dryopithecus indicus* but the current consensus is to use Gregory *et al*'s (1938) designation as *S. indicus*.

Specimen courtesy of Yale Peabody Museum

Sivapithecus sivalensis Lyddekker, 1879

Note that Figures 3.40–3.42 are of specimens that were assigned to *Ramapithecus punjabicus* and figured prominently in discussions of early hominid (in the sense of undoubted human ancestors) evolution: ". . . we do consider it highly probable (say, a 75% likelihood) that *Ramapithecus* is ancestral to later Cenozoic hominids" (Simons and Pilbeam, 1978:152).

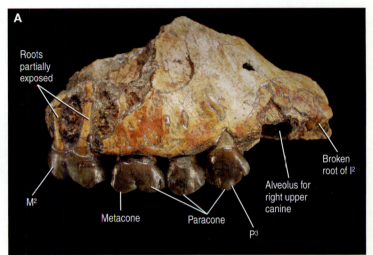

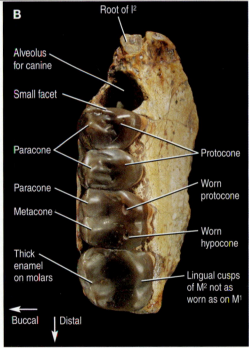

3.40 Famous YPM.VP.013799, designated by Lewis (1934) as the holotype of *Ramapithecus brevirostris* (nomenclature retained by Simons, 1961) and later (Simons, 1964; Simons and Pilbeam, 1965) referred to *R. punjabicus*. **A** Buccal view. **B** Occlusal view. The specimen was collected by G.E. Lewis on Aug. 9, 1932, 1/2 mile east of Chakrana and 4 miles east of Hari Talyangar, in sediments dated as late Middle Siwalik. The maxillary fragment was figured (Pilbeam, 1972; Simons, 1961, 1968) and reconstructed in a hypothetical reconstruction of the face with YPM VP.013814 (Simons, 1968). Simons (1968) and Simons and Pilbeam (1978) interpreted this individual as having diverging rather than parallel tooth rows, reduction of facial prognathism, a canine in which the transverse width is greater than the mesiodistal length, and small incisors and canines—features that would have implied hominin status.

Specimen courtesy of Yale Peabody Museum

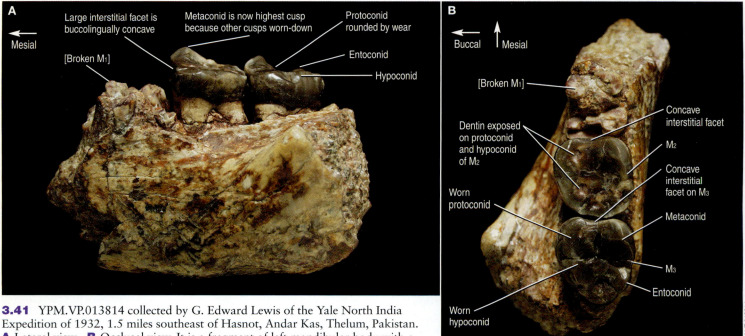

3.41 YPM.VP.013814 collected by G. Edward Lewis of the Yale North India Expedition of 1932, 1.5 miles southeast of Hasnot, Andar Kas, Thelum, Pakistan. **A** Lateral view. **B** Occlusal view. It is a fragment of left mandibular body with a portion of the root of P$_4$, broken M$_1$, and intact M$_{2-3}$. It was originally the holotype of Lewis's (1934) *Bramapithecus thorpei*, later assigned to *Ramapithecus punjabicus* by Simons and Pilbeam (1965) , and now referred to *S. sivalensis* (Ward and Brown, 1986). Pilbeam (1972) states that, during his research with Simons, they noticed that all specimens assigned to *Bramapithecus* were mandibles but all of the *Ramapithecus* specimens were maxilla; they then decided that the upper and lower jaw fragments belonged to the same species *Ramapithecus punjabicus*.   Specimen courtesy of Yale Peabody Museum

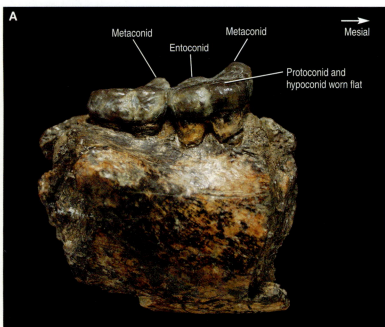

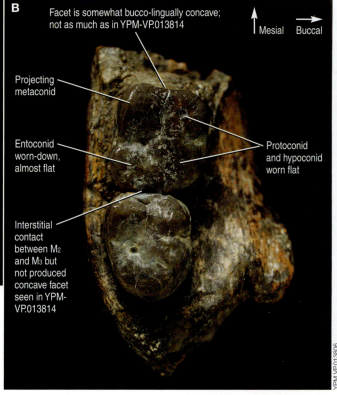

3.42 Fragment of right lower mandible with M$_{2-3}$. Lewis (1934) designated this specimen as the holotype of *Dryopithecus sivalensis*. **A** Buccal aspect. **B** Occlusal aspect. It was collected on July 27, 1932 by the Yale North India Expedition at Haritalyangar, India, in the Nagri Formation. Simons and Pilbeam (1965) later included it in the hypodigm of *Ramapithecus punjabicus* and recently it has been referred to *S. sivalensis* (Ward and Brown, 1986).   Specimen courtesy of Yale Peabody Museum

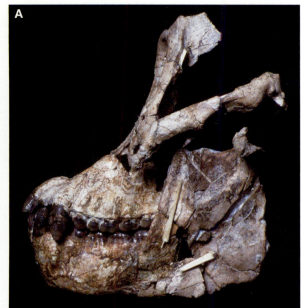

A

B

3.43 Facial skeleton with mandible of GSP 15000 from the Potwar Plateau, Pakistan. **A** Left lateral view. **B** Right oblique view. The specimen is identified as *S. sivalensis* by Kelley (2002) although it has also been referred to *S. indicus* (Pilbeam, 1982). The specimen includes the upper face, palate and mandible. There is a complete adult dentition. Pilbeam (1982) describes the morphology. The face is concave in lateral profile. The supraorbital tori are small. The frontal profile is steep. There is no frontal sinus. The orbits are oval and there is a narrow interorbital region. The midfacial length is long. Upper incisors are strongly procumbent. Pilbeam (1982) favorably compares the mandibular fossa to that of the orangutan. The mandible is deep and robust with high, vertical rami. Pilbeam (1982:234) concludes ". . . in facial profile, jaw joint morphology, malar morphology, orbital shape and disposition, and overall palatal shape, the specimen is quite orang-like. In other features the two species differ: for example in tooth morphology and wear, and in the considerable fossil midfacial length and ramus height."

Courtesy of Dr. David Pilbeam

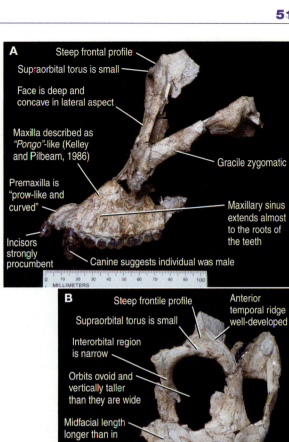

A
- Steep frontal profile
- Supraorbital torus is small
- Face is deep and concave in lateral aspect
- Maxilla described as *"Pongo"*-like (Kelley and Pilbeam, 1986)
- Premaxilla is "prow-like and curved"
- Incisors strongly procumbent
- Gracile zygomatic
- Maxillary sinus extends almost to the roots of the teeth
- Canine suggests individual was male

B
- Steep frontile profile
- Supraorbital torus is small
- Anterior temporal ridge well-developed
- Interorbital region is narrow
- Orbits ovoid and vertically taller than they are wide
- Midfacial length longer than in chimpanzee or orangutan
- Triangular nasal aperture

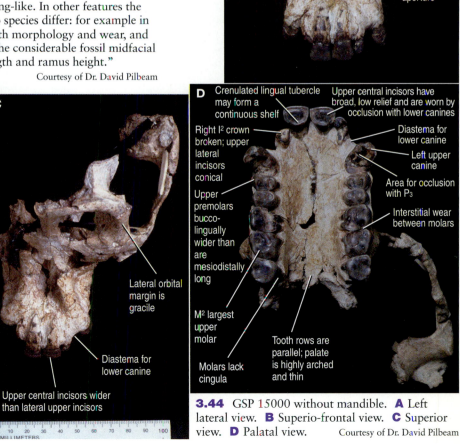

C
- Lateral orbital margin is gracile
- Diastema for lower canine
- Upper central incisors wider than lateral upper incisors

D
- Crenulated lingual tubercle may form a continuous shelf
- Upper central incisors have broad, low relief and are worn by occlusion with lower canines
- Right I² crown broken; upper lateral incisors conical
- Diastema for lower canine
- Left upper canine
- Area for occlusion with P₃
- Upper premolars bucco-lingually wider than are mesiodistally long
- Interstitial wear between molars
- M² largest upper molar
- Molars lack cingula
- Tooth rows are parallel; palate is highly arched and thin

3.44 GSP 15000 without mandible. **A** Left lateral view. **B** Superio-frontal view. **C** Superior view. **D** Palatal view. Courtesy of Dr. David Pilbeam

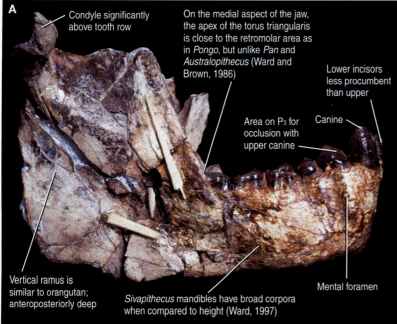

A

Condyle significantly above tooth row

On the medial aspect of the jaw, the apex of the torus triangularis is close to the retromolar area as in *Pongo*, but unlike *Pan* and *Australopithecus* (Ward and Brown, 1986)

Lower incisors less procumbent than upper

Area on P₃ for occlusion with upper canine

Canine

Vertical ramus is similar to orangutan; anteroposteriorly deep

Sivapithecus mandibles have broad corpora when compared to height (Ward, 1997)

Mental foramen

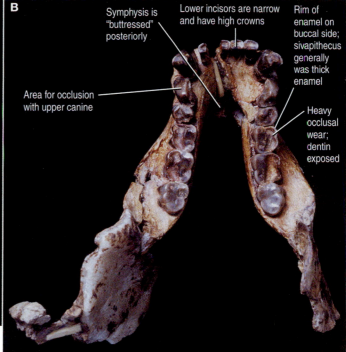

B

Symphysis is "buttressed" posteriorly

Lower incisors are narrow and have high crowns

Rim of enamel on buccal side; sivapithecus generally was thick enamel

Area for occlusion with upper canine

Heavy occlusal wear; dentin exposed

3.45 Mandible of GSP 15000. **A** Lateral view. **B** Occlusal view.

Courtesy of Dr. David Pilbeam

Comparison of *Rangwapithecus gordoni* and *Oreopithecus bambolii*

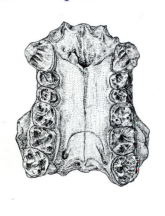

3.46 Drawings from casts of upper dentitions of KNM-RU 700 *Rangwapithecus gordoni* (left) from Songhor, Kenya and an adult female *Oreopithecus bambolii* (right) from Casteana, Toscana, Italy. *R. gordoni* is dated to the early Miocene (20–19 Ma) and *O. bambolii* to the later Miocene (7–6 Ma). Harrison (2002) assigns *Rangwapithecus* to the new subfamily Nyanzapithecinae of the family Proconsulidae with *Nyanzapithecus, Mabokopithecus,* and *Turkanapithecus.* Begun (2002) places *O. bambolii* as the only species within the subfamily Oreopithecinae of the Hominidae. In both taxa, there is a staggered appearance to the arrangement of the upper molar cusps, so that the apex of the paracone is mesial to the apex of the protocone, and the apex of the metacone is mesial to the apex of the hypocone. The incisors are missing in the *R. gordoni*, the canines are broken but are stout, and both P³ and P⁴ are bicuspid with well-developed paracone and protocone although the former is more projecting. The lingual cusps on M¹ were worn-down before the buccal cusps and M¹ may have exposed dentin before M³ has started to wear (Simons, Andrews, and Pilbeam, 1978). There are lingual cingula on the upper molars. Upper molars increase in size from M¹–M³. In the *Oreopithecus*, I² is smaller and more pointed than I¹. I² has a pronounced lingual cingulum. P⁴ is bicuspid with paracone and protocone.

Courtesy of Paul F. Whitehead

Oreopithecus bambolii Gervais, 1872

Begun (2002):

Order Primates Linnaeus, 1758
Infraorder Catarrhini É. Geoffroy Saint-Hilaire, 1812
Superfamily Hominoidea Gray, 1825
Family Hominidae Gray, 1825
Subfamily Oreopithecinae Schwalbe, 1915
Genus and Species *Oreopithecus bambolii* Gervais, 1872

3.47 Photograph of a cast of the slab of the 1958 specimen in its slab. Begun (2002:361) states that, "The bulk of the evidence suggests that *Oreopithecus* is the most primitive known great ape." Problems with the interpretation of the material partially stem from the fact that the species appears to be a mixture of characters that are similar to modern apes but also others that are either primitive or are actually autapomorphies that are homoplasious with characters in other species (Begun, 2002; Harrison, 1986; Moyà-Solà and Köhler, 1997).

Courtesy of and © copyright by Dr. Eric Delson

Graecopithecus freybergi or Ouranopithecus macedoniensis?

Begun (2002) assigns *G. freybergi* to a subfamily *incertae sedis* of the Family Hominidae, and *O. macedoniensis* to the Tribe Dryopithecini of the Hominidae.

Geological Range: 8–6.6 Ma for genus Graecopithecus; 9 Ma for O. macedoniensis

3.48 Frontal view of skull of a large mid-Miocene ape from Greece. Its combination of well-developed brow ridges, wide-spaced orbits and jaw shape may suggest affinities to the *Pan-Gorilla-Homo* clade (Jolly and White, 1995). Begun (2002) points-out that the genus is difficult to distinguish from other Miocene hominoids, including *Sivapithecus, Ankarapithecus,* and *Ouranopithecus* and assigns (p. 355) the depicted skull to the latter genus.

Courtesy of and copyright © Dr. Eric Delson

Lufengpithecus lufengensis Xu et al, 1978

Kelley (2002):

Order Primates Linnaeus, 1758
Infraorder Catarrhini É. Geoffroy Saint-Hilaire, 1812
  Superfamily Hominoidea Gray, 1825
    Family Hominidae Gray, 1825
      Subfamily Ponginae Elliot, 1913
        Tribe Lufengpithecini
          Genus and Species *Lufengpithecus lufengensis* Xu *et al*, 1978

Geological Age: Late Miocene

3.49 Superior view of crushed skull PA 644. The genus is from the late Miocene of Yunnan Province, China. Kelley (2002) describes the molars as possessing relatively thick enamel, peripheralized cusp apices and large basins, and crenulations on occlusal surfaces. Both upper and lower incisors are high-crowned. The orbits are square in outline and the interorbital region is wide. Noteworthy is that the superior margin of the nasal aperture is higher than are the inferior margins of the orbits. The nasoalveolar clivus is described as short.

Courtesy of and copyright
© Dr. Eric Delson

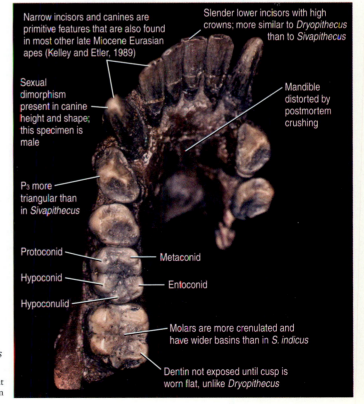

Narrow incisors and canines are primitive features that are also found in most other late Miocene Eurasian apes (Kelley and Etler, 1989)

Slender lower incisors with high crowns; more similar to *Dryopithecus* than to *Sivapithecus*

Sexual dimorphism present in canine height and shape; this specimen is male

Mandible distorted by postmortem crushing

P₃ more triangular than in *Sivapithecus*

Protoconid
Metaconid

Hypoconid
Entoconid

Hypoconulid

Molars are more crenulated and have wider basins than in *S. indicus*

Dentin not exposed until cusp is worn flat, unlike *Dryopithecus*

3.50 Occlusal view of mandible of *Lufengpithecus lufengensis*.

Courtesy of and copyright
© Dr. Eric Delson

Sahelanthropus tchadensis Brunet et al, 2002

Brunet *et al* (2002):

Order Primates Linnaeus, 1758
Suborder Anthropoidea Mivart, 1864
   Superfamily Hominoidea Gray, 1825
    Family Hominidae Gray, 1825
     Genus and species *Sahelanthropus tchadensis* Brunet *et al*, 2002

Geological Date: 6–7 Ma

3.51 Left oblique view of the almost complete skull (TM 266-01-060-1), holotype, from the Toros-Menalla area of the Djurab Desert of northern Chad. Faunal dating of the site suggests a Late Miocene date for the site (6–7 Ma). Brunet *et al* (2002:145) view the species as the "oldest known member of the hominid clade." They describe the skull as possessing a long and narrow basicranium, large canine fossa, small U-shaped dental arcade, flat frontal squama, large external occipital crest, small occipital condyles, short basi-occipital, relatively small incisors, molars with low rounded cusps, and enamel thickness of cheek teeth intermediate between the chimpanzee and *Australopithecus*. They conclude (2002: 51) that, "*Sahelanthropus* is the oldest and most primitive known member of the hominid clade, close to the divergence of hominids and chimpanzees."

Copyright © M.P.F.T.

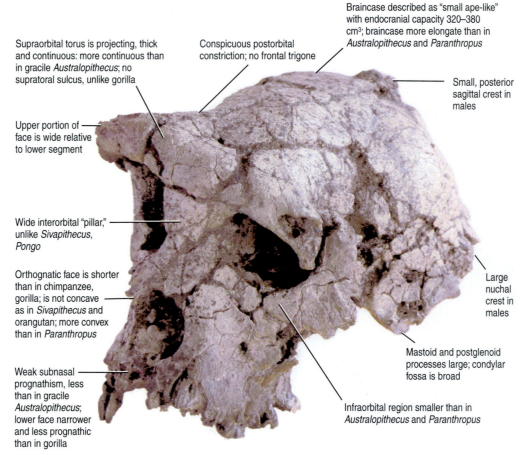

Supraorbital torus is projecting, thick and continuous: more continuous than in gracile *Australopithecus*; no supratoral sulcus, unlike gorilla

Conspicuous postorbital constriction; no frontal trigone

Braincase described as "small ape-like" with endocranial capacity 320–380 cm³; braincase more elongate than in *Australopithecus* and *Paranthropus*

Small, posterior sagittal crest in males

Upper portion of face is wide relative to lower segment

Wide interorbital "pillar," unlike *Sivapithecus*, *Pongo*

Orthognatic face is shorter than in chimpanzee, gorilla; is not concave as in *Sivapithecus* and orangutan; more convex than in *Paranthropus*

Weak subnasal prognathism, less than in gracile *Australopithecus*; lower face narrower and less prognathic than in gorilla

Large nuchal crest in males

Mastoid and postglenoid processes large; condylar fossa is broad

Infraorbital region smaller than in *Australopithecus* and *Paranthropus*

AUSTRALOPITHECINE FOSSILS

Comparative Aspects of the Australopithecine Skull

TABLE 3.1 COMPARISON OF SELECTED FEATURES IN *A. AFRICANUS* AND *P. ROBUSTUS*

FEATURE	A. africanus	P. robustus
Cranial capacity	Small, 425-485cc; mean 440cc	Small, 530cc
Cranial build	Lightly constructed, long, ovoid	Robust, spheroidal crania vault
Pneumatization of skull	Moderate	Substantial
Postorbital constriction	Moderate	Strong
Sagittal crest	Absent or rare; if present, then limited	Present in both males and females
Relation of inferior temporal line to superior nuchal line[1]	Separated (compound temporal/nuchal crest absent)	Commonly separated
Cranial base	Expanded	Shortened
Relation of vault to upper margin of orbits	Elevated above margins	Rises only slightly above upper margins
Configuration of face	Moderately to substantially prognathous, moderately flat surface	Broad, not markedly elongated, surface is flat or concave, nasal aperture and nasal bones set in a midfacial hollow.
Zygomatic arch	Moderately developed	Strongly developed
Ramus of mandible	Moderate height, slopes posteriorly	High, vertical in orientation

[1] Rak (1983) documents the presence of the compound T/N crest in two specimens of *A. afarensis* AL-162-28 and AL-333-45 and in *P. boisei* specimens OH-5, Omo 323, and L-338-Y6 but not in the "hyperrobust" KNM-ER 406.

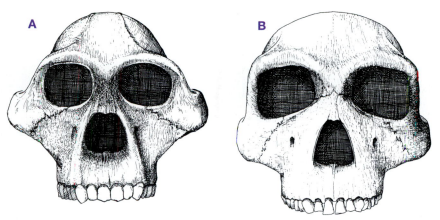

3.52 Idealized composite drawings of the facial masks. **A** *Australopithecus africanus.* **B** *Homo habilis.* From *The Australopithecine Face,* Figure 7, page 127, by Yoel Rak, copyright © 1983, Elsevier Science (USA). Reproduced by permission of Academic Press.

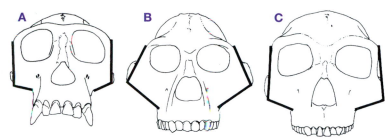

3.54 Outlines of the facial mask. **A** *Pan troglodytes.* **B** *A. africanus.* **C** *Homo.* The chimpanzee and *Homo* have basically square facial outlines compared to the gracile australopithecine, where the outline converges from the widest point toward the midline both superiorly and inferiorly.
From *The Australopithecine Face,* Figure 12, page 132, by Yoel Rak, copyright © 1983, Elsevier Science (USA). Reproduced by permission of Academic Press.

3.55 Comparison of facial masks, depicting some salient morphological features. **A** *A. africanus.* **B** *P. robustus.* a) The *zygomatic prominence* is the anterolateral flaring of the infraorbital region on the transverse plane. A pronounced prominence is produced in *A. africanus,* which is distinguishable from the flat vertical plate of chimpanzees, gorillas, *H. sapiens,* and *H. habilis* (SK-847, KNM-ER 3733). In *P. robustus,* the zygomatic prominence is elongated because of the greater height of the zygomatic bone than in *A. africanus.* b) The *anterior pillars* are found on the right and left sides of the nasal aperture. It is suggested that the development of the anterior pillars is a product of the molarization of the premolars in *A. africanus* and (even further in) *P. robustus* and serve to resist increased chewing forces. c) The *maxillary furrow* is a form of the canine fossa which is formed by the junction of the infraorbital bone surface and the anterior pillar. Rak (1983:13) describes it as assuming "the shape of a corner extending upward along the anterior pillar as far as the pillar is discernible." In *P. robustus,* the infraorbital area has a distinctive feature called the *maxillary trigon* bounded by the anterior pillar and zygomaticomaxillary step, and concave in transverse section. The canine fossa is the primitive condition in this area, exemplified by *A. afarensis.* It is altered into the maxillary furrow in *A. africanus* and the maxillary fossula in *P. robustus.* d) A *nasoalveolar triangular frame* is a triangular, elevated structure that is differentiated from the flat, level surface of the remainder of the face in *A. africanus.* The feature is not found in modern *H. sapiens,* KNM-ER 1805, nor in the gorilla and chimpanzee. Specimens such as KNM-ER 1470 and 3733, SK-847 and OH-24, while different from other *Homo,* do not have the configuration found in *A. africanus.* e) The *zygomaticomaxillary step* is a raised ridge at the zygomaticomaxillary suture found in *P. robustus.* f) The *zygomaticomaxillary fossa* is a deep pit that interrupts the continuity of the zygomaticomaxillary step in *P. robustus.* g) In *P. robustus,* the *nasoalveolar gutter* is a depressed area between the anterior pillars that grades into the floor of the nasal cavity (Aiello and Dean, 1990). Rak (1983) notes that there is a similarity in this region to the gorilla but believes that there are different functional derivations. He argues that the more marked withdrawal of the palate in *P. robustus* than in *A. africanus* causes the nasoalveolar triangular frame of the latter to become the nasoalveolar gutter of the former. h) The *maxillary fossula* is a fovea found inferior to the infraorbital foramen in *P. robustus.* The infraorbital foramen is low on the anterior surface of the maxilla near to the inferomedial corner of the maxillary trigon. The bone surface of the maxillary trigon separates the maxillary fossula from the infraorbital foramen and is called the *subforamen divide.*

From *The Australopithecine Face,* Figure 8, page 128 (top), and Figure 16, page 135 (bottom), by Yoel Rak, copyright © 1983, Elsevier Science (USA). Reproduced by permission of Academic Press.

3.53 The region of the lateral orbital margin in A) an adult *Pan troglodytes* and B) *A. africanus.* The root of the temporal process is near to the vertical plane of the lateral orbital margin in the chimpanzee, but it projects significantly lateral to the vertical plane in *A. africanus.* The width of the root of the frontal process is "achieved by the deviation of the inner margins medially" in the chimpanzee, but is "achieved additionally by the deviation of the outer margins laterally" in *A. africanus* (Rak, 1983: 129). See Figure 3.70 (STS-5).

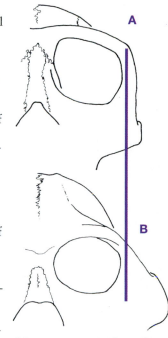

From *The Australopithecine Face,* Figure 9, page 129, by Yoel Rak, copyright © 1983, Elsevier Science (USA). Reproduced by permission of Academic Press.

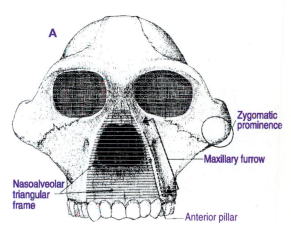

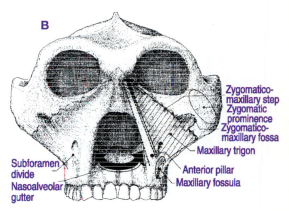

A — Zygomatic prominence / Maxillary furrow / Nasoalveolar triangular frame / Anterior pillar

B — Zygomatico-maxillary step / Zygomatic prominence / Zygomatico-maxillary fossa / Maxillary trigon / Anterior pillar / Maxillary fossula / Subforamen divide / Nasoalveolar gutter

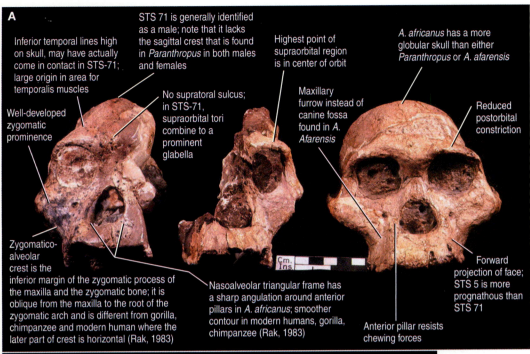

A

Inferior temporal lines high on skull, may have actually come in contact in STS-71; large origin in area for temporalis muscles

STS 71 is generally identified as a male; note that it lacks the sagittal crest that is found in *Paranthropus* in both males and females

Highest point of supraorbital region is in center of orbit

A. africanus has a more globular skull than either *Paranthropus* or *A. afarensis*

Well-developed zygomatic prominence

No supratoral sulcus; in STS-71, supraorbital tori combine to a prominent glabella

Maxillary furrow instead of canine fossa found in *A. Afarensis*

Reduced postorbital constriction

Zygomatico-alveolar crest is the inferior margin of the zygomatic process of the maxilla and the zygomatic bone; it is oblique from the maxilla to the root of the zygomatic arch and is different from gorilla, chimpanzee and modern human where the later part of crest is horizontal (Rak, 1983)

Nasoalveolar triangular frame has a sharp angulation around anterior pillars in *A. africanus*; smoother contour in modern humans, gorilla, chimpanzee (Rak, 1983)

Anterior pillar resists chewing forces

Forward projection of face; STS 5 is more prognathous than STS 71

3.56 Comparison of the face in australopithecines. **A** Gracile australopithecines from Sterkfontein. **B** The "robust australopithecines" (paranthropines) from Swartkrans.

Courtesy of and copyright © Dr. Eric Delson

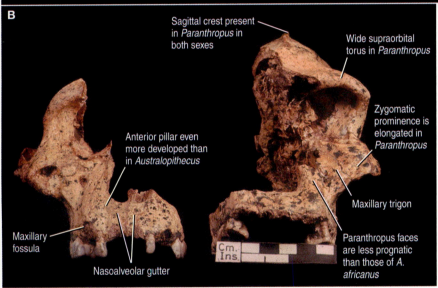

B

Sagittal crest present in *Paranthropus* in both sexes

Wide supraorbital torus in *Paranthropus*

Anterior pillar even more developed than in *Australopithecus*

Zygomatic prominence is elongated in *Paranthropus*

Maxillary trigon

Maxillary fossula

Nasoalveolar gutter

Paranthropus faces are less prognatic than those of *A. africanus*

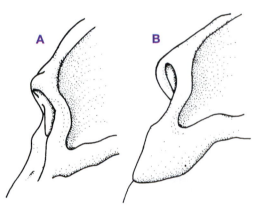

A   **B**

3.57 Comparison of the face. **A** *A. africanus*. **B** *P. robustus*. The glabellar region has a convex protruding anterior profile in the robust australopithecine (paranthropine) in contrast to the concave contour of the lateral margin of its orbit.

From *The Australopithecine Face*, Figure 17, page 136, by Yoel Rak, copyright © 1983, Elsevier Science (USA). Reproduced by permission of Academic Press.

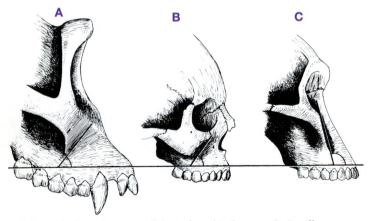

A   **B**   **C**

3.58 Right lateral aspect of the infraorbital area. **A** Gorilla. **B** Modern *Homo sapiens*. **C** *A. africanus*. There are differences in the relationships of the infraorbital area to the alveolar plane (horizontal line) and to the anterior profile.

From *The Australopithecine Face*, Figure 14, page 133, by Yoel Rak, copyright © 1983, Elsevier Science (USA). Reproduced by permission of Academic Press.

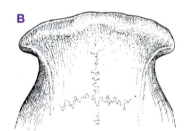
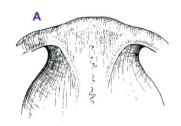

A   **B**

3.59 Comparison of the supraorbital region and frontal squama. **A** *A. africanus*. **B** *Homo*. The postorbital constriction is more pronounced in the australopithecine. The temporal crests are confined to the medial walls of the temporal fossa in *Homo* but are closer together on the superior surface of the skull in *A. africanus*, causing the supraorbital region to become "a laterally flaring bar" (Rak, 1983:134).   From *The Australopithecine Face*, Figure 15, page 134, by Yoel Rak, copyright © 1983, Elsevier Science (USA). Reproduced by permission of Academic Press.

Map of Plio-Pleistocene Australopithecine/Paranthropine Sites

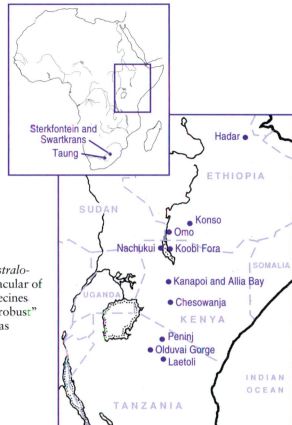

3.60 Map of major fossil sites for *Australopithecus* and *Paranthropus*. In the vernacular of physical anthropology, the australopithecines are divided into the "gracile" and the "robust" forms (some workers refer to the latter as paranthropines).

TABLE 3.2 TAXONOMIC SYNONYMS USED FOR AUSTRALOPITHECINES[1,2]

SPECIES	SYNONYMS	AGE (MA)	SITES	REPRESENTATIVE SPECIMENS
Ardipithecus ramidus	*Australopithecus ramidus*, *Australopithecus praegens*	5.8-4.39	Saitune Dora, Alayba, Asa Koma, Digiba Dora, Kuseralee Dora, Amba, Sagantole, Aramis (Ethiopia)	ARA-VP-6/1
Australopithecus afarensis	*Preanthropus africanus*, *Meganthropus africanus*	3.7-2.6	Kanapoi, West Turkana, Koobi Fora (Kenya); Laetoli (Tanzania); Belodelie, Maka, Fejej, Hadar (Ethiopia)	A.L. 288-1 "Lucy", A.L. 400-1, L.H. 4
Australopithecus africanus	*Australopithecus transvaalensis*, *Plesianthropus transvaalensis*, *Australopithecus prometheus*	3.0-2.0	Taung, Sterkfontein, Makapansgat (South Africa)	Taung infant, Sts 5, Sts 14, STS 52, STS 71
Paranthropus aethiopicus	*Australopithecus aethiopicus*, *Paraustralopithecus aethiopicus*	2.8-2.2	Omo (Ethiopia); West Turkana (Kenya)	KNM-WT 17000
Paranthropus boisei	*Australopithecus boisei*, *Zinjanthropus boisei*	2.3-1.2	Olduvai Gorge, Peninj (Tanzania); Chesowanja, Koobi Fora, West Turkana (Kenya); Omo (Ethiopia)	O.H. 5 ("Zinj"), KNM-ER 406
Paranthropus robustus	*Australopithecus robustus*, *Paranthropus crassidens*, *Australopithecus crassidens*	c. 1.7 (White, 2002); 2.0-1.0 and (Jolly and White, 1995)	Swartkrans, Kromdraai, Drimolen Gondolin (South Africa)	SK 23, SK 47, SK 48, SK 50

[1] The genus name for the "robust" australopithecines employed here is *Paranthropus* because it appears to be commonly employed in the recent literature, although both Jolly and White (1995) and White (2002) continue to use *Australopithecus* for both "gracile" and "robust" forms.
[2] Other described australopithecine taxa include *Australopithecus anamensis* and *Australopithecus garhi*.

Australopithecus afarensis Johanson *et al* (1978)

Geological Range: 3.6–2.9 Ma

3.61 Anterior view of the skeleton of AL 188, the famous "Lucy" skeleton. Johanson and Edey (1981) recount its discovery and analysis; see Johanson *et al* (1982) for detailed description. The examination of specific anatomical characters was important in the understanding of its significance in human evolution. The presence of a femur and proximal tibia allowed Johanson and his colleagues to conclude that the bicondylar angle is more similar to that of a modern human than it is to a chimpanzee. Other workers have reached different conclusions about the nature of locomotor adaptations in *A. afarensis* (see below). For example, Aiello and Dean (1990) write that the tibia and fibula show a mosaic morphology, with a tibial plateau that is similar to a chimpanzee but a distal tibial articular surface that is perpendicular to the long axis of the bone as in a modern human. The fact that it included many postcranial elements also allowed reconstruction of its bodily proportions. Jungers (1982:676) concluded that the species "had attained forelimb proportions similar to those of modern humans but possessed hindlimbs that were relatively much shorter . . .", as reflected by a humerofemoral index that is between modern humans and great apes. He concludes that the species may have been bipedal but it was not the same as modern human bipedalism because of a shorter relative stride length, higher energetic cost of walking and lower gait velocity.

Institute of Human Origins and National Museum of Ethiopia

A. afarensis has compound temporal nuchal crest similar to chimpanzee; crest is not present in *A. africanus*

Cranial capacity intermediate between chimpanzee and human

Upper portion of face is small but lower part is prognathous; this is similar to ape

Naso-alveolar clivus is convex; it is flatter and straighter in *A. africanus*

Canine fossa is deep

A. afarensis shows pneumatization of temporal squama similar to an ape; but it is in the mastoid area in *A. africanus*

Canine roots large so they cause a bulge in upper jaw; this is also true in apes but not humans

3.62 Right lateral view of skull of *A. afarensis*, A.L. 444-2. The specimen was discovered by Dr. Yoel Rak in 1992, and is believed to be about 3 million years old. Areas in yellow are reconstructed. Noteworthy is the large size of the canines and that the incisors are larger relative to the posterior teeth than in later hominins. It is stated that the frontal is similar to one collected at Belohdeli, Ethiopia dated to 3.9 Ma and attributed to the same species.

Institute of Human Origins and National Museum of Ethiopia

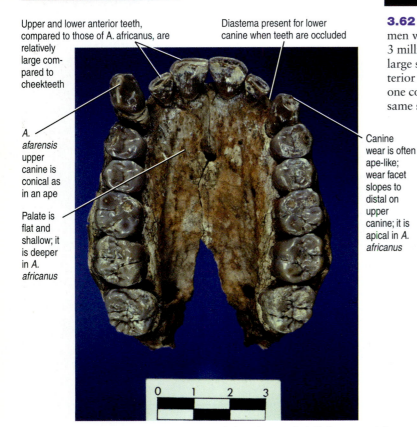

Upper and lower anterior teeth, compared to those of *A. africanus*, are relatively large compared to cheekteeth

Diastema present for lower canine when teeth are occluded

A. afarensis upper canine is conical as in an ape

Palate is flat and shallow; it is deeper in *A. africanus*

Canine wear is often ape-like; wear facet slopes to distal on upper canine; it is apical in *A. africanus*

3.63 Occlusal view of A.L. 200-1a, adult palate with full dentition. The stratigraphic placement of the specimen is SH-1.

Institute of Human Origins and National Museum of Ethiopia

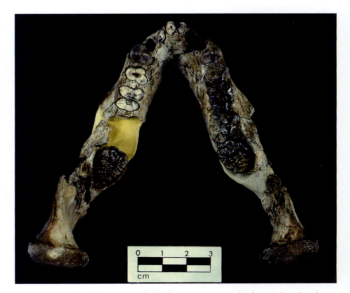

3.64 Occlusal aspect of the lower jaw with the right cheek-teeth, broken incisor crowns, and left P3 and M3 (A.L. 288-1i). See Johanson *et al* (1982) for detailed description.

Institute of Human Origins and National Museum of Ethiopia

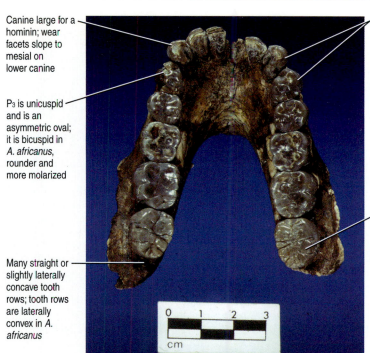

Canine large for a hominin; wear facets slope to mesial on lower canine

P₃ is unicuspid and is an asymmetric oval; it is bicuspid in *A. africanus*, rounder and more molarized

When teeth are worn, lower canine and P₃ project above tooth row; in *A. africanus*, all teeth are worn flat

Many straight or slightly laterally concave tooth rows; tooth rows are laterally convex in *A. africanus*

Molars increase in size from M₁ to M₃; in *A. africanus*, M₂ is the largest

3.65 Occlusal aspect of the partial mandible (A.L. 400-1a) and almost complete dentition. The right I₁ is broken and the left P₃ is damaged on the buccal side.

Institute of Human Origins and National Museum of Ethiopia

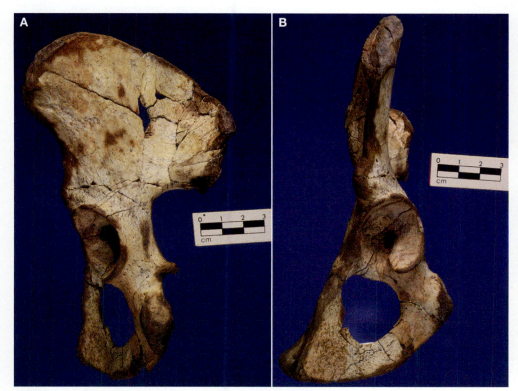

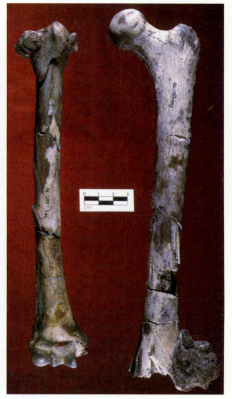

3.66 A.L. 288-1ao, left innominate from the "Lucy" skeleton. **A** Lateral aspect. **B** Anterior aspect. This is one of the best preserved australopithecine pelvic bones. There has been controversy surrounding the interpretation of its features in regard to the nature of *A. afarensis* bipedality. Stern and Susman (1983) report that the acetabulum is more similar to that of African apes than to modern humans, in contrast to the interpretation of the pelvis of STS 14 (see below). The ilium is considered to be identical to that of *A. africanus* (McHenry, 1982, 1986).

Institute of Human Origins and National Museum of Ethiopia

3.67 Right humerus (A.L. 288-1m, two pieces) on left and left femur (A.L. 288-1ap) on right from "Lucy." The general proportions of the australopithecine/paranthropine proximal femur are different from those of both humans and chimpanzees, with a greater relative length of the neck.

Institute of Human Origins and National Museum of Ethiopia

Paranthropus aethiopicus Arambourg and Coppens (1968)
Geological Range: c. 2.7–c. 2.3 Ma
KNM-WT 17000

3.68 The "Black Skull," KNM-WT 17000.
A Left lateral view. **B** Frontal view. Note
the very prognathic face, more than in other
paranthropines such as WT 17400. The
specimen has a long basioccipital. There are
compound temporal and nuchal crests. It has
a longer, less rounded zygomatic profile than
other paranthropines. There is a pronounced
postorbital constriction. The "dishing" of the
face is apparent in lateral profile. Glabella is
prominent, and the supraorbital torus arches
over each orbit and descends to meet glabella
at the midline (Aiello and Dean, 1990).

Copyright © National Museums of Kenya

Australopithecus africanus Dart, 1925
Geological Range: 3–2 Ma
Taung

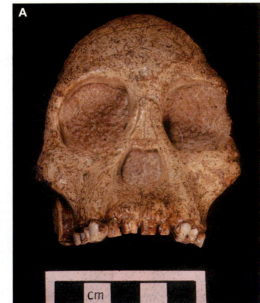

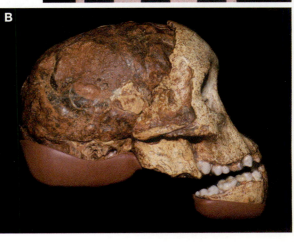

3.69 The famous Taung skull, the type specimen of *A. africanus*.
A Frontal view. **B** Right lateral view. The frontal view is without the
mandible. The specimen is estimated to be upper Pliocene (2.5 Ma) in
age, but it is difficult to precisely date the fossil because it comes from
a South African cave deposit. See Dart (1959), Clark (1967) and
Reader (1988) for accounts of the discovery and early study of the *A.
africanus*. Estimates of the age of the individual vary from 3–6 years
old, depending on how quickly australopithecines matured. The position of the foramen magnum suggested to Dart (1959) that the individual was bipedal and therefore a hominin. The cranium is rounded
and the juvenile brain size was probably 405–410 cc and would have
been about 440 cc as an adult (Day, 1977).

Courtesy of and copyright © Dr. Eric Delson

STS-5

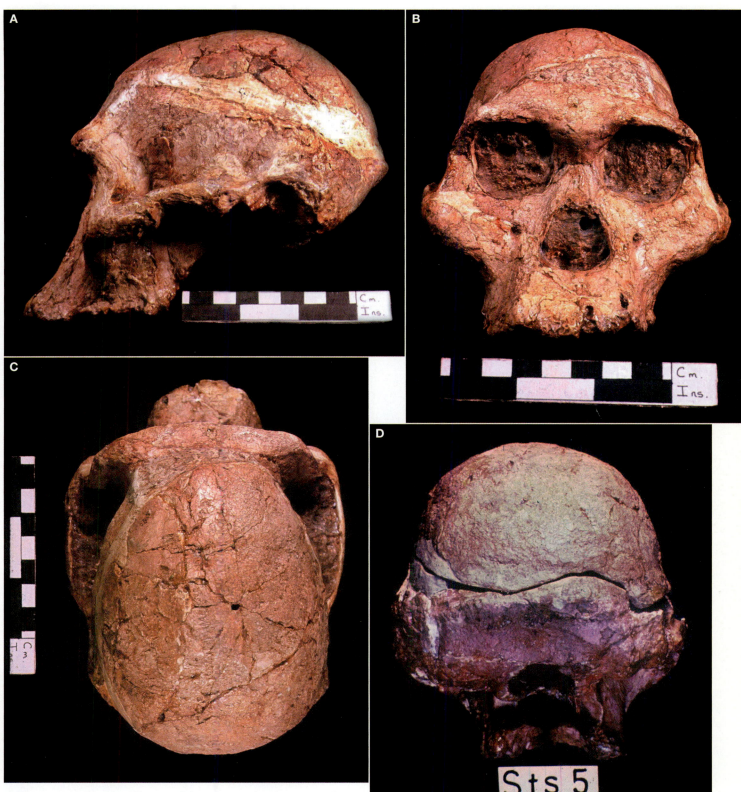

3.70 Sts 5, "Mrs. Ples" from Sterkfontein, South Africa. **A** Left lateral view. **B** Frontal view. **C** Superior view. **D** Posterior view, STS 5, "Mrs. Ples" housed at the Transvaal Museum, South Africa. The skull is believed to be upper Pliocene, 2.3–2.8 Ma. It's brain size is estimated to be 485 cc.

Specimens A, B, and C courtesy of and Copyright © Dr. Eric Delson,
Specimen D, STS 5, "Mes. Ples" housed at the Transvaal Museum, South Africa

STS-52

A	B	C

3.71 A Right lateral aspect of articulated maxilla (STS 52a) and mandible (STS 52b). **B** Occlusal views of maxilla (left) and mandible (right).
C Close-up occlusal view of maxilla. The specimen is assigned to the same geological age as STS 5. It lacks the large canine and diastema that
were present in *A. afarensis*, but the cheekteeth are large.   Courtesy of and copyright © Dr. Eric Delson

STS-71

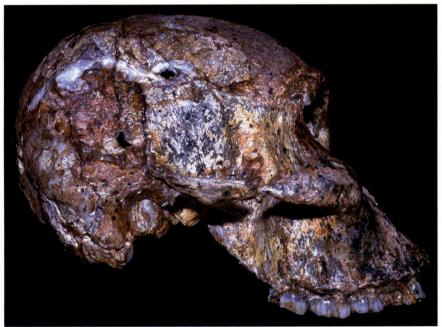

3.72 Right lateral aspect of skull of Sts
71. It is estimated to be 2.3–2.8 Ma in age.
The cranial capacity is estimated to be 428
cc, although it is not as primitive in morphology as that of *A. afarensis*. Tattersall
and Schwartz (2000) consider both Sts 52
and 71 to be shorter-faced than StW 252,
and hypothesize that more than individuals
of more than one species may have been
falsely grouped together in *A. africanus*.

Courtesy of and copyright © Dr. Eric Delson

STS-14

3.73 Medial (left) and lateral (right) views of innominates of
STS 14, also 2.3–2.8 Ma in age. This is one of the most complete australopithecine pelvic bones. In contrast to *A. afarensis*,
the acetabulum is interpreted as more human-like than ape-
like: relative to acetabular diameter, the depth, notch width
and thickness of the walls are in the human range of variation
(Aiello and Dean, 1990; Schultz, 1969). It has other characters
that are similar to modern humans: short, wide ilium, well-
developed sciatic notch, prominent anterior inferior iliac spine,
and a short ischium. However, it has some other features that
are different from modern humans: relatively small acetabular
joint surfaces, flared iliac blade and relatively small iliac tuberosity. The question is not whether australopithecines were
bipedal (most people would agree they were) but whether their
bipedalism was the same as in modern humans (Aiello and
Dean, 1990).   Courtesy of and copyright © Dr. Eric Delson

Paranthropus boisei Leakey, 1959

Geological Range: c. 2.3–c. 1.4 Ma

KNM-ER 406

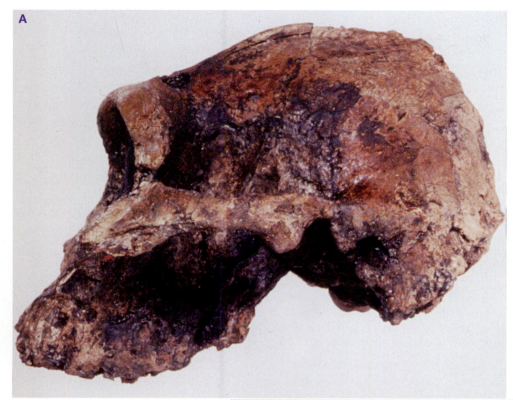

A

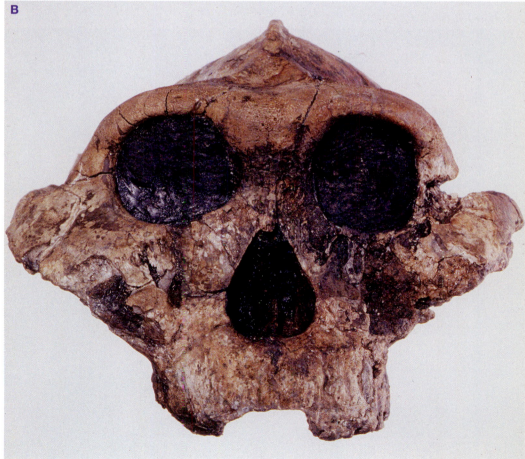

B

3.74 KNM-ER 406. **A** Left lateral view. **B** Frontal view. The specimen is from Ileret, East Turkana, Kenya and is about 1.5 Ma in age.

KNM-ER 732

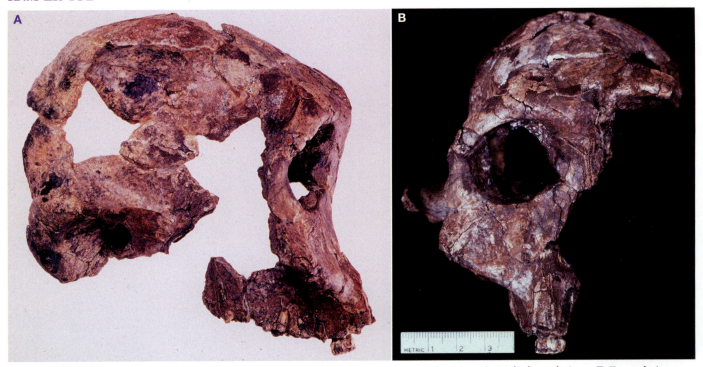

3.75 KNM-ER 732 from Ileret, East Turkana, Kenya; it is the same age as KNM-ER 406. **A** Right lateral view. **B** Frontal view. The specimen was discovered by Leakey in 1970. The skull is smaller than that of the famous "Zinjanthropus" and does not have a sagittal crest. Brain size is estimated at 550 cc. It is dated to about 1.7 million years. Copyright © National Museums of Kenya

Paranthropus robustus **Broom, 1938**

Geological Range: c. 1.7 Ma

SK 48 and SK 23

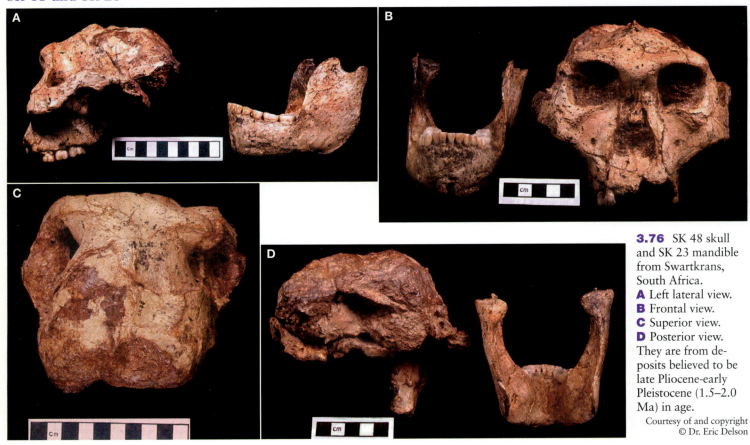

3.76 SK 48 skull and SK 23 mandible from Swartkrans, South Africa. **A** Left lateral view. **B** Frontal view. **C** Superior view. **D** Posterior view. They are from deposits believed to be late Pliocene-early Pleistocene (1.5–2.0 Ma) in age.

Courtesy of and copyright © Dr. Eric Delson

SK 23 and STS-52b

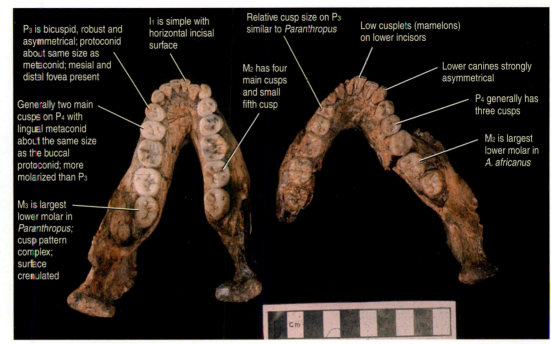

P₃ is bicuspid, robust and asymmetrical; protoconid about same size as metaconid; mesial and distal fovea present

I₁ is simple with horizontal incisal surface

Relative cusp size on P₃ similar to *Paranthropus*

Low cusplets (mamelons) on lower incisors

Generally two main cusps on P₄ with lingual metaconid about the same size as the buccal protoconid; more molarized than P₃

M₂ has four main cusps and small fifth cusp

Lower canines strongly asymmetrical

P₄ generally has three cusps

M₂ is largest lower molar in *A. africanus*

M₃ is largest lower molar in *Paranthropus*; cusp pattern complex; surface crenulated

3.77 Comparison of lower jaw and dentition of *P. robustus* (left, SK 23) and *A. africanus* (right, STS 52b). Note that the dental arcades cannot be compared in shape because of postmortem distortion in both specimens. Note the robustness of the SK 23 mandible.

Courtesy of and copyright © Dr. Eric Delson

Postcrania of P. robustus

3.78 Right innominate (SK 50), proximal femora (SK 97 and SK 82) and distal right humerus from Swartkrans. The material is generally assigned to *P. robustus*, although it is not definitely associated with any specific cranial or dental material from the site. The innominate is distorted by crushing and pieces are missing. *P. robustus* has a wider iliac blade, that projects above the auricular surface further, than in *A. africanus* and the auricular surface is relatively larger (Aiello and Dean, 1990). The humerus may be a cercopithecid (Delson, pers. comm.).

Courtesy of and copyright © Dr. Eric Delson

HOMO FOSSILS

Homo habilis Leakey *et al*, 1964

Dunsworth and Walker (2002) define *Homo habilis* as possessing a mean cranial capacity greater than *Australopithecus* but smaller than *H. erectus*; smaller mandibles and maxillae than those of *Australopithecus*; nascent occipital torus; coronal chord greater than sagittal chord in the parietals; midface breadth less than upper face breadth; nasal margins sharp and everted nasal sill; premolars narrower than in *Australopithecus*; molar size in the lower range of *Australopithecus*; buccolingual narrowing and mesiodistal elongation of all teeth, particularly lower cheekteeth.

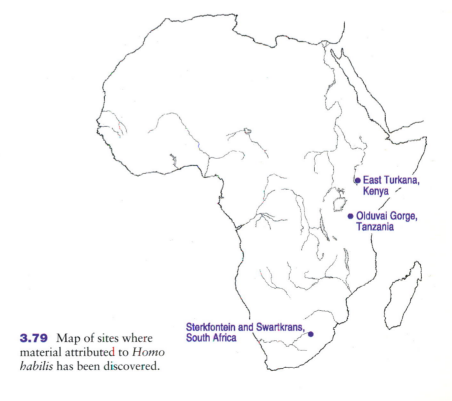

East Turkana, Kenya

Olduvai Gorge, Tanzania

Sterkfontein and Swartkrans, South Africa

3.79 Map of sites where material attributed to *Homo habilis* has been discovered.

KNM-ER 1805

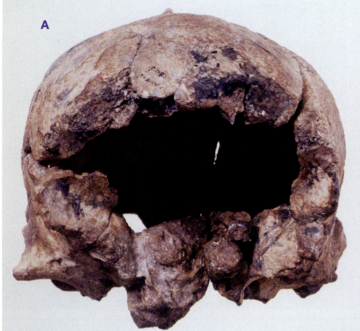

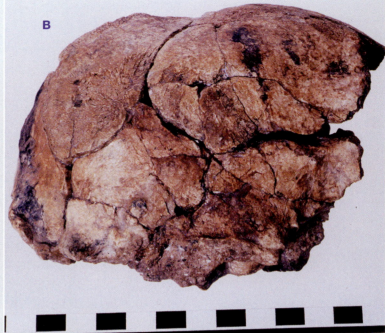

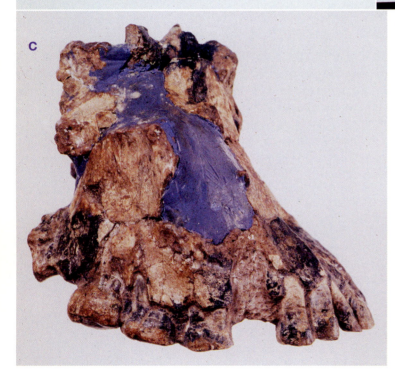

3.80 Skull from Koobi Fora, East Turkana, Kenya. **A** Frontal view of the skull without face. **B** Right lateral aspect of skull. **C** Right oblique aspect of maxilla. The specimen is regarded as early Pleistocene in age. The specimen was discovered by Abell in 1973. It is estimated to be 1.85 million years old. Cranial capacity is estimated to be 600 cc. It has a sagittal crest but its teeth are small, so Wood (1991) has assigned it to *H. habilis* but Prat (2002) suggests that it is a paranthropine (robust australopithecine).

SK 847

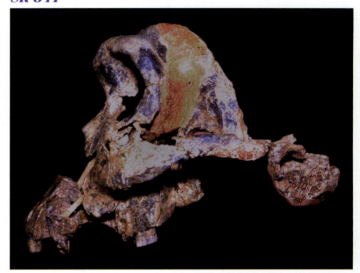

3.81 Left lateral aspect of face and partial cranium. The specimen is from Member 1 at Swartkrans, South Africa. On the basis of the fauna, Members 1–3 are believed to span 1.8–1.0 Ma (Brain, 1993). SK 847 is generally attributed to early *Homo*. Clarke (1977) assigned it to *Homo* sp., then affiliated it with KNM-ER 3733 in a species which he called *Homo leakeyi*.

KNM-ER 1813

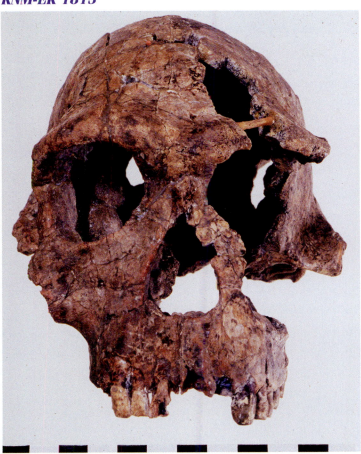

KNM-ER 1470 Homo rudolfensis?

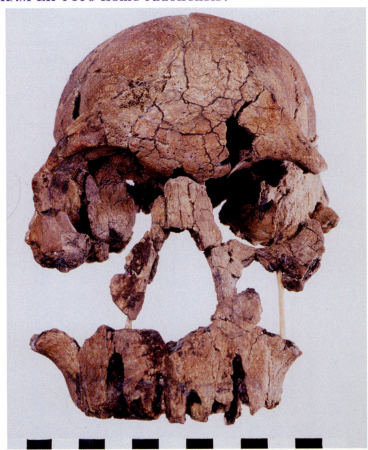

3.82 Frontal view of skull from Koobi Fora, East Turkana, Kenya discovered by Kimeu in 1973. The specimen is believed to be from 1.8 Ma. Holloway (2000) derives a cranial capacity of 510 ml for the specimen. It is broadly similar to KNM-ER 1470 but is smaller.

Copyright © National Museums of Kenya

3.83 Frontal aspect of skull from Koobi Fora, East Turkana, Kenya, judged to be 1.9 million years old. The specimen was described by Day *et al* (1975) and assigned to *H. habilis* by Howell (1978). Later, Wood (1992) and Leakey *et al* (2001) termed it the type specimen of *H. rudolfensis*. Holloway (2000) estimates a cranial capacity of 752 ml. Day *et al* (1975) described the skull as a long ovoid with a moderate postorbital constriction. The supraorbital ridges were not considered to be particularly projecting, but the frontal air sinus was characterized as "enormously developed." In the face, the nasoalveolar clivus is almost flat, there is little subnasal prognathism, midface breadth is greater than upper face breadth. Dunsworth and Walker (2002) distinguish it from *H. habilis* because of a larger cranial capacity, less everted nasal margins, and relatively larger upper anterior dental alveoli.

Copyright © National Museums of Kenya

Homo erectus (Dubois, 1892)

3.84 Map of sites of material generally attributed to *Homo erectus*.

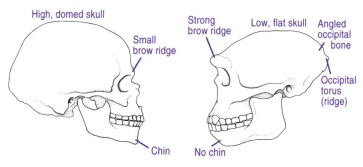

3.85 Idealized comparison of Paleolithic *H. sapiens* (left) with *H. erectus* (right) from Stringer and Gamble (1993:65).

In Search of the Neanderthals by C. Stringer and Gamble. Copyright © 1993. Reprinted by permission of Thames and Hudson.

KNM-WT 15000 *Homo ergaster?*

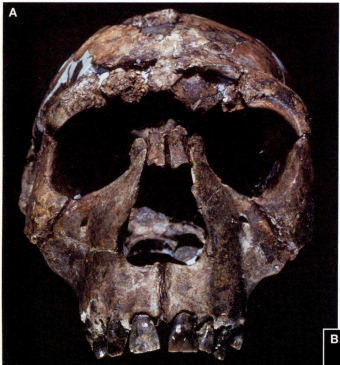

TABLE 3.3 SOME GENERAL CHARACTERISTICS OF THE SKULL OF *HOMO ERECTUS*

CHARACTER	STATE FOUND GENERALLY IN *H. ERECTUS*
Cranial shape	Long, relatively low in outline
Endocranial volume	Average is close to 1,000ml
Basicranial axis	Flattened in comparison to more flexed base of anatomically modern *H. sapiens*
Facial skeleton	Robust
Alveolar prognathism	Pronounced
Nasal aperture	Relatively broad; nasoalveolar clivus flat
Brow ridges	Heavy
Supratoral sulci	Shallow or absent
Frontal bone	Profile is flat; midline keeling common
Postorbital narrowing	Marked
Placement of maximum cranial breadth	At level of supramastoid crest (toward the base of the skull)
Thickness of cranial bones	Almost twice as thick as in modern humans
Occipital bone	Strongly flexed; no true occipital protuberance; strongly developed transverse occipital torus
Mandible	Large, robust; long dental arcade; ramus is very broad; external symphyseal profile is receding (no chin); large bicondylar breadth

Adapted from Rightmire, 1990 and Dunsworth and Walker, 2002.

3.86 Skull Nariokotome III from West Turkana, Kenya. **A** Frontal view. **B** Left lateral view. The skull is from a skeleton that is 80% complete and dates to the early Pleistocene (1.51–1.56 Ma). The frontal view is without the mandible. The various authors in Walker and Leakey (1993a) present a detailed description and analysis of the site, geological setting and age, taphonomy, associated fauna, and morphology of the specimen. Walker and Leakey (1993) report on the skull in detail. Despite the fact that the skull was found in about 70 pieces, it is almost complete but is missing portions of the superior surface of the cranial vault and of the basicranium. The brain size was estimated at about 880 cc, which would place it below the mean for *H. erectus* from East Africa, Indonesia, and China (Begun and Walker, 1993). Walker (1993) discusses the fossil in the context of other East African finds, especially the type for *H. ergaster* KNM-ER-992, and concludes (p. 421) "If . . . the early African *erectus*-grade hominids need their own taxon, then *H. ergaster* is the appropriate name for it." He would include KNM-ER 992, KNM-WT 15000, KNM-ER 820 and KNM-ER 730 in this taxon on basis of morphology of the lower dentition.   Copyright © National Museums of Kenya

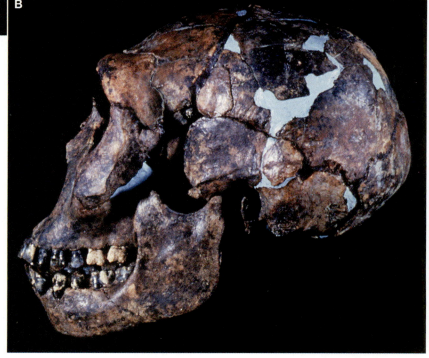

KNM-ER 3733 Homo ergaster?

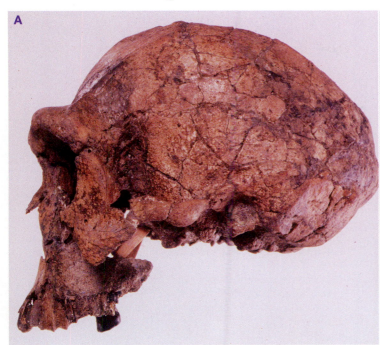

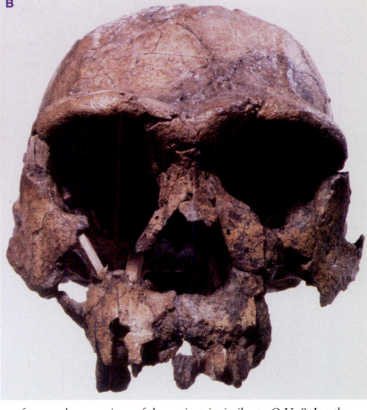

3.87 Skull from Koobi Fora, East Turkana, Kenya, early Pleistocene (1.8 Ma) in age. **A** Left lateral view. **B** Frontal view. The specimen was described by Leakey and Walker (1976). Rightmire (1990) enumerates features that are similar to *H. erectus*: prominent keeling in frontal midline, with frontal flattened on either side of midline; marked postorbital constriction; shelving of supraorbital torus; cranial profile is low; form and proportions of the occiput is similar to O.H. 9. In other characters, it is more similar to *H. sapiens*, particularly in certain aspects of the basicranium. The supraorbital torus is thinner than on O.H. 9 and glabella is less massive.

"Meganthropus"   ## *Sangiran 4*

3.88 Buccal view of fragment of right mandibular body from Sangiran, central Java, Indonesia. The specimen was originally designated *Meganthropus palaeojavanicus* by Weidenreich (1945). Lovejoy (1970) then assigned it to *H. erectus*. The date of the find is controversial because it is not possible to determine a radiometric date. Note the mental foramen in buccal view. The roots of the cheekteeth are partially exposed.

3.89 Right lateral aspect of Sangiran 4. The large mastoid process and the external auditory meatus are present in the specimen. The specimen is large and robust. Holloway (1981) provides a cranial capacity of 908 ml. Rightmire (1990) describes it as possessing a keel along the midline to lambda, as well as parasagittal flattening, that are not found in the Turkana *Homo erectus*. The bone of the occiput is thick and there is a well-developed occipital torus which is shelf-like superiorly.

Comparison of Sangiran 2 with Olduvai Hominid 9

3.90 A Left lateral comparison of O.H. 9 **B** with Sangiran 2. O.H. 9 is from LLK, upper bed II, Olduvai Gorge, Tanzania and is probably about 1.25 million years old. It may be a male. Rightmire (1990) assigned O.H. 9 to *H. erectus,* Tattersall and Schwartz (2000) later called it *H. habilis.* Schwartz and Tattersall (2003) refer it to the "OH 9 Morph." Sangiran 2, which is smaller than some other specimens from the locality and may be a female, is either from the Grenzbank or upper Pucangan (Rightmire, 1990) or Kabuh (Schwartz and Tattersall, 2002) Formations. There has been disagreement about the age of the deposits, with Schwartz and Tattersall (2002) prefering a range of 1.5–1.0 Ma for almost all of the hominin fossils. While there has been considerable heterogeneity in the taxonomic terms applied to the Sangiran fossils, most workers consider Sangiran 2 to be *H. erectus.* Holloway (1975, 1981) provides a cranial capacity of about 813 ml for Sangiran 2 and 1,067 ml for O.H. 9.

Courtesy of Dr. G. Phillip Rightmire

O.H. 9, Sangiran 2, Trinil 2

3.91 Superior view of O.H. 9 (left), Sangiran 2 (center), and Trinil 2 (right). The Trinil 2 calotte shows damage to the brows and only a small section of the supraorbital torus on the left. However, it is apparent that there is significant postorbital constriction, no appreciable supratoral sulcus, the vault is flattened behind vertex, there is some blunt keeling along the midline, a prominent bregmatic eminence, and a straight torus on the occiput; parasagittal flattening of the vault is greater than in the smaller Sangiran specimens such as Sangiran 2 (Rightmire, 1990). In O.H. 9, the supraorbital tori are massive, their superior surfaces are broad and "shelf-like," they merge centrally with with a huge glabellar eminence, and there is a shallow supratoral sulcus on each side. In Sangiran 2, part of the supraorbital torus is present on the left, as well as the supraorbital rim, but glabella is missing. The skull is a little smaller than Trinil 2, but the thickness of the vault bones is close to that of Trinil 2. Rightmire (1990) writes that the postorbital constriction is as developed as in Trinil 2. The supratoral shelf is flattened. Left and center photos by C. Tarka, courtesy and © National Museum of Tanzania (Dar es Salaam), Naturmuseum Senckenberg (Frankfurt) and Dr. Eric Delson; right, courtesy of and © Dr. Eric Delson

Homo erectus from Zhoukoudian, People's Republic of China

The history of the collection and study of fossils from the cave site of Zhoukoudian is provided by Shapiro (1974) and Wu and Poirier (1995). The most detailed studies were published by Franz Weidenreich from 1936–1943, including the monographs of *Palaeontologia Sinica* from which the following illustrations were obtained. Five skulls, teeth, mandibles and postcranial bones were discovered at Loc. 1, dated to between 220,00–580,000 years (Etler, 1996). Wu and Poirier (1995) refer the skulls to *H.e. pekinensis*.

Figures 3.92-3.96 present the cranial material Wu and Poirier (1995) and Etler (1996) summarize the morphology. The skulls are dolichocranial. The greatest width of the skull is at its base and the breadth decreases as one moves to the top of the skull. The forehead is sloping but has a bump on the frontal squama. The skull vault is flat. The cranial capacity is about two-thirds that of modern humans. The supraorbital tori are heavy, projecting and continuous and there is a supraorbital sulcus. The postorbital constriction is marked. There is a more central rather than backward position of the foramen magnum. There is a sharp angle between the upper and lower parts of the occipital bone. There is a sagittal prominence, a well-developed occipital torus, frontal torus, angular torus. The transverse cranial vault contour is described as "bell-shaped." Cortical bone thickness is marked.

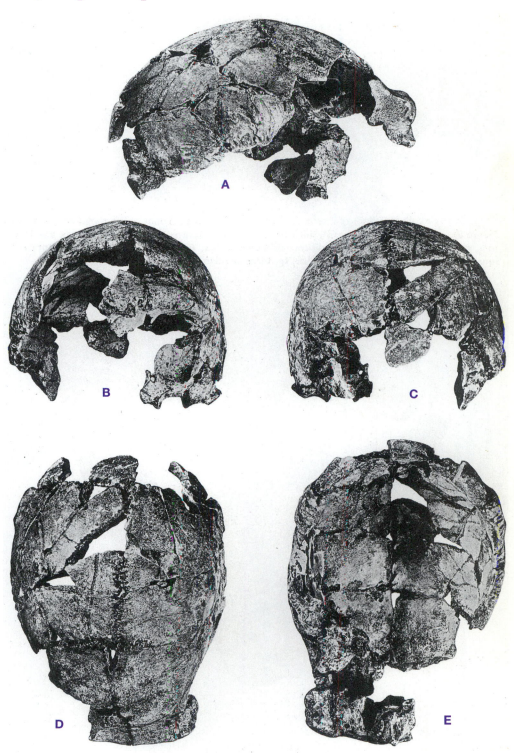

3.92 Photographs of "Sinanthropus" Skull II—Skull of Locus D. **A** Right lateral. **B** Frontal. **0C** Posterior. **D** Superior. **E** Inferior.

Courtesy of the Institute of Vertebrate Paleontology and Paleoanthropology, People's Republic of China

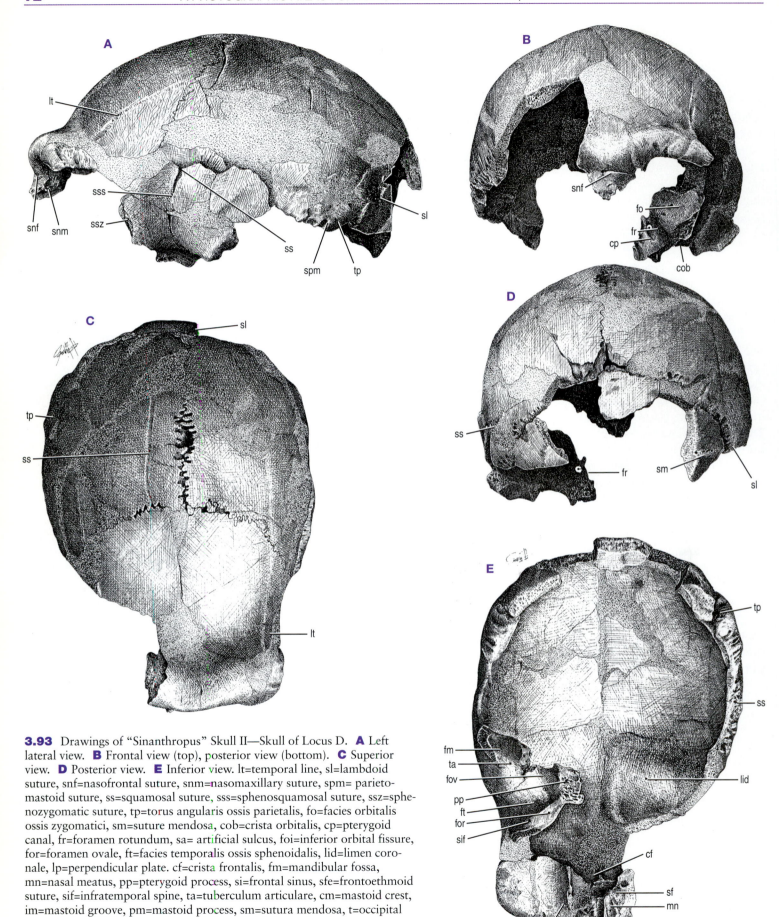

3.93 Drawings of "Sinanthropus" Skull II—Skull of Locus D. **A** Left lateral view. **B** Frontal view (top), posterior view (bottom). **C** Superior view. **D** Posterior view. **E** Inferior view. lt=temporal line, sl=lambdoid suture, snf=nasofrontal suture, snm=nasomaxillary suture, spm= parieto-mastoid suture, ss=squamosal suture, sss=sphenosquamosal suture, ssz=sphe-nozygomatic suture, tp=torus angularis ossis parietalis, fo=facies orbitalis ossis zygomatici, sm=suture mendosa, cob=crista orbitalis, cp=pterygoid canal, fr=foramen rotundum, sa= artificial sulcus, foi=inferior orbital fissure, for=foramen ovale, ft=facies temporalis ossis sphenoidalis, lid=limen coro-nale, lp=perpendicular plate. cf=crista frontalis, fm=mandibular fossa, mn=nasal meatus, pp=pterygoid process, si=frontal sinus, sfe=frontoethmoid suture, sif=infratemporal spine, ta=tuberculum articulare, cm=mastoid crest, im=mastoid groove, pm=mastoid process, sm=sutura mendosa, t=occipital torus, da1=artificial depression 1, da2=artificial depression 2.

Courtesy of the Institute of Vertebrate Paleontology and Paleoanthropology,
People's Republic of China

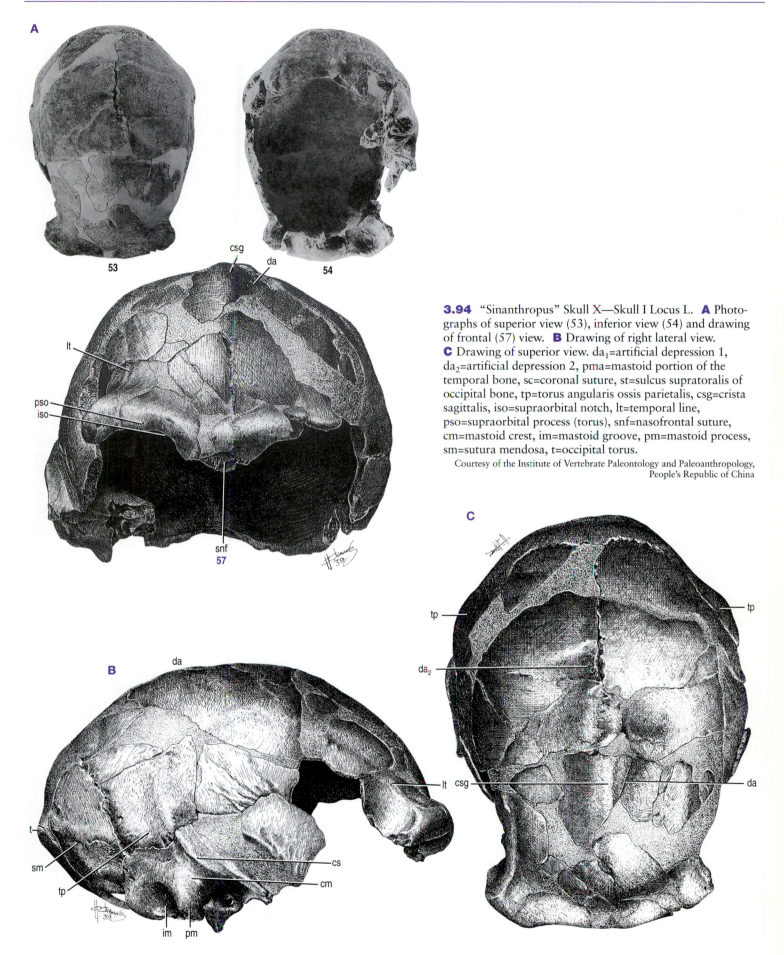

A

53

54

csg

da

3.94 "Sinanthropus" Skull X—Skull I Locus L. **A** Photographs of superior view (53), inferior view (54) and drawing of frontal (57) view. **B** Drawing of right lateral view. **C** Drawing of superior view. da$_1$=artificial depression 1, da$_2$=artificial depression 2, pma=mastoid portion of the temporal bone, sc=coronal suture, st=sulcus supratoralis of occipital bone, tp=torus angularis ossis parietalis, csg=crista sagittalis, iso=supraorbital notch, lt=temporal line, pso=supraorbital process (torus), snf=nasofrontal suture, cm=mastoid crest, im=mastoid groove, pm=mastoid process, sm=sutura mendosa, t=occipital torus.

Courtesy of the Institute of Vertebrate Paleontology and Paleoanthropology, People's Republic of China

lt

pso
iso

snf
57

B

da

t

sm

tp

im   pm

cs

cm

C

tp

tp

da$_2$

csg

da

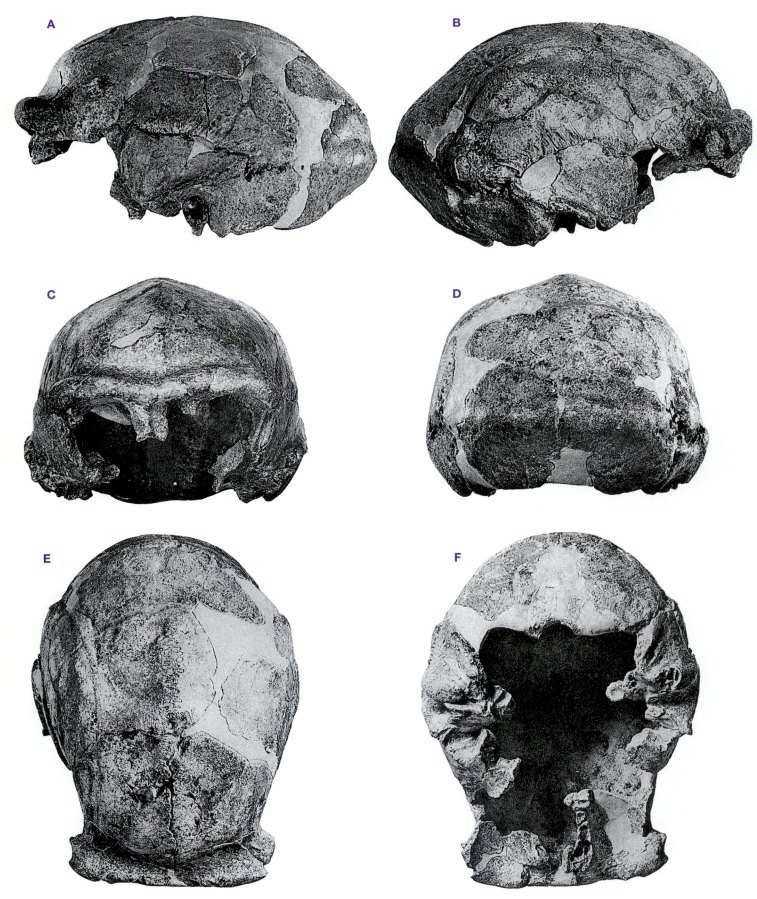

3.95 "Sinanthropus" Skull XI—Skull II Locus L. **A** Left lateral view. **B** Right lateral view. **C** Frontal view. **D** Posterior view. **E** Superior aspect. **F** Inferior aspect.

Courtesy of the Institute of Vertebrate Paleontology and Paleoanthropology, People's Republic of China

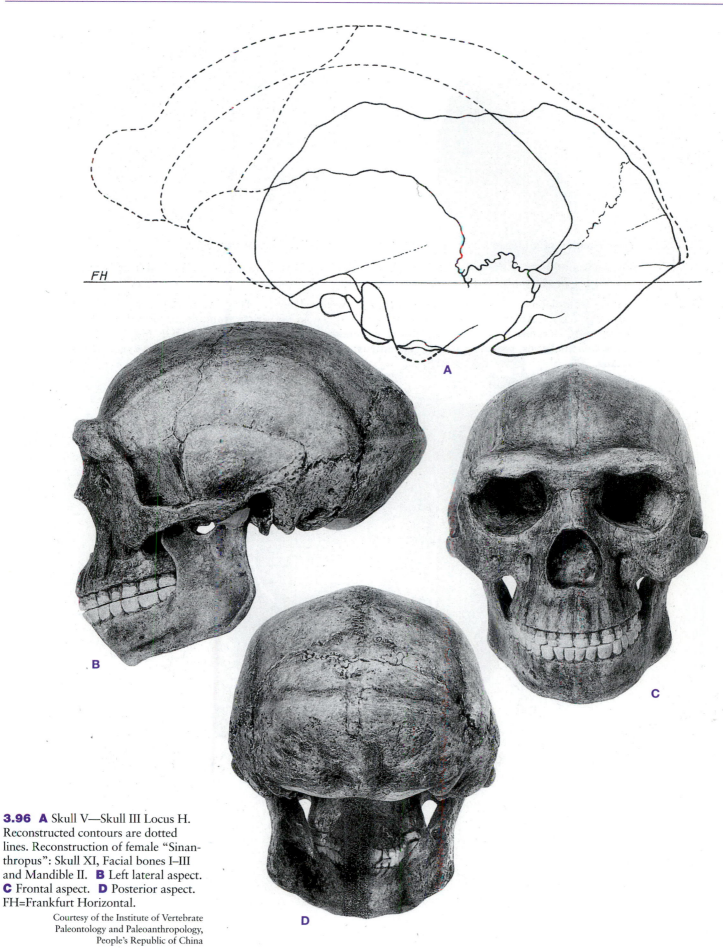

3.96 A Skull V—Skull III Locus H. Reconstructed contours are dotted lines. Reconstruction of female "Sinanthropus": Skull XI, Facial bones I–III and Mandible II. **B** Left lateral aspect. **C** Frontal aspect. **D** Posterior aspect. FH=Frankfurt Horizontal.

Courtesy of the Institute of Vertebrate Paleontology and Paleoanthropology, People's Republic of China

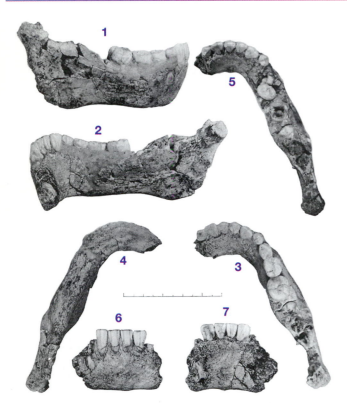

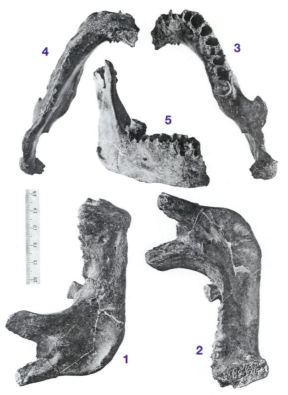

3.97 Photographs of fragments of the right side of the "Sinan-thropus" female child mandible from Locus B (BI) partly re-stored. 1=buccal, 2-lingual, 3=occlusal, 4=inferior, 5=occlusal view of specimen in stage of restoration showing the unerupted permanent premolars *in situ*, 6=labial view of symphyseal frag-ment, 7=lingual view of symphyseal fragment.

Courtesy of the Institute of Vertebrate Paleontology and Paleoanthropology,
People's Republic of China

3.98 Views of the left side and symphysis of an adult female "Sinanthropus" mandible from Locus H ("Sinanthropus" jaw H I) recovered in 1935. 1=buccal, 2=lingual, 3=occlusal, 4=inferior, 5=anterior. Mandibles from the site are robust and do not have chins. The ramus is broad and there is a deep masseteric fossa (Etler, 1996).

Courtesy of the Institute of Vertebrate Paleontology and Paleoanthropology,
People's Republic of China

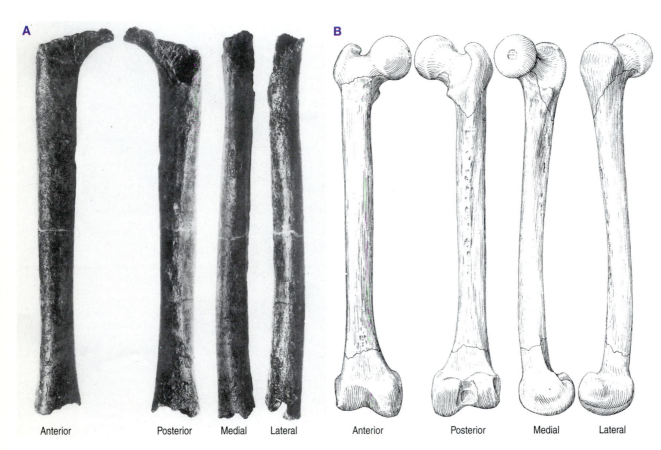

| Anterior | Posterior | Medial | Lateral | Anterior | Posterior | Medial | Lateral |

3.99 A Photo-graphs of "Sinan-thropus" Femur IV (MII) right femur of an adult male individual.
B Reconstructions of the same right femur. The femora are robust, with thick compact bone walls, narrow medullary cavity and transverse flattening of the bone shaft (*platymeria*).

Courtesy of the Institute of Vertebrate Paleontology and Paleoanthropology, People's Republic of China

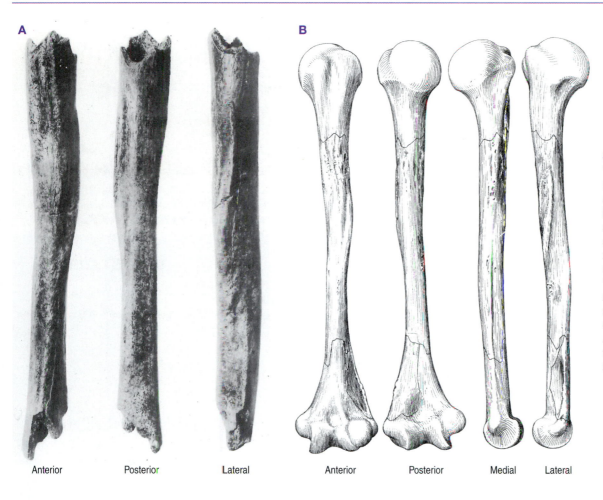

A Anterior   Posterior   Lateral   **B** Anterior   Posterior   Medial   Lateral

3.100 Photographs of "Sinanthropus" Humerus II (JIII). **A** Left humerus of an adult male individual. **B** Reconstructions of the same humerus. The proximal and distal epiphyses are missing. Wu and Poirier (1995:57–59) describe the "size, proportion, shape, and muscular markings of the shaft are identical to those of modern humans, but the *H. erectus* humerus has a thicker wall and a narrower medullary canal [cavity]."

Courtesy of the Institute of Vertebrate Paleontology and Paleoanthropology, People's Republic of China

Sambungmacan 3

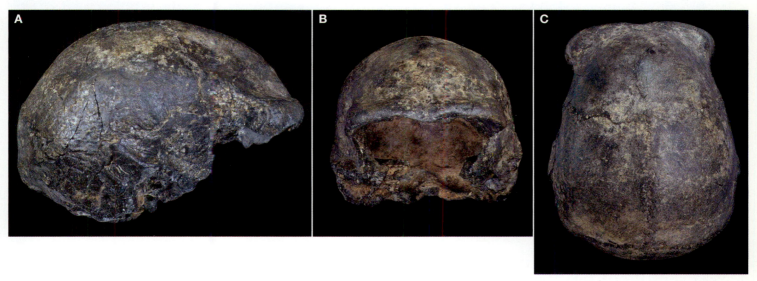

3.101 SM 3 (also known as Poloyo 1) is an adult skull, lacking the facial and basicranial regions, presumably from a sandbar in the Solo River, Central Java, Indonesia, but actually of uncertain provenance. Schwartz and Tattersall (2003) suppose that it may be about 200,000 years old; Delson *et al* (2001) cautiously suggest that the specimen is somewhere between 100,00-1 million years old. **A** Right lateral view. **B** Frontal View. **C** Superior view. The specimen was studied by Delson *et al* (2001) using a three- dimensional geometric morphometric and comparative morphological analysis to compare it to casts of *H. erectus* and "archaic" *H. sapiens* and 10 modern human skulls. The study concludes that the specimen is the most similar to the Ngandong and Sambungmacan1 material and generally similar to Trinil 2 and the Sangiran fossils. It is, therefore, placed within *H. erectus*. It is unique in comparison to the sample in that the supratoral plane is more vertical and glabella more anteriorly projecting on the frontal bone, and the occipital angle is less acute.

Courtesy of and copyright © Dr. Eric Delson

Middle Pleistocene Hominins: "Archaic" *Homo sapiens* or *Homo heidelbergensis?*

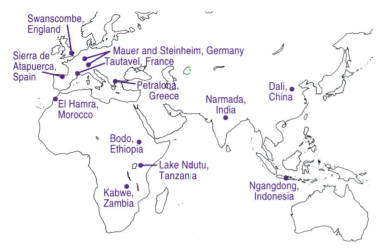

3.102 Map of major sites of Middle Pleistocene hominid discoveries.

Comparison of a Possible H. erectus with "Early Archaic H. sapiens"

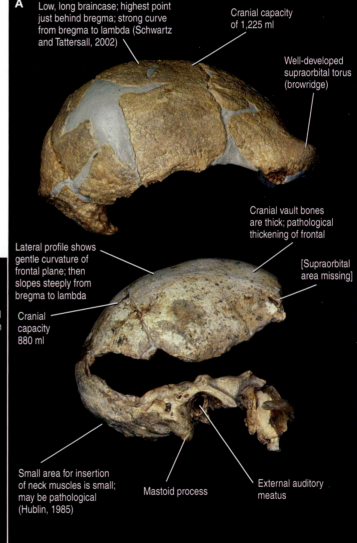

A Low, long braincase; highest point just behind bregma; strong curve from bregma to lambda (Schwartz and Tattersall, 2002)

Cranial capacity of 1,225 ml

Well-developed supraorbital torus (browridge)

Cranial vault bones are thick; pathological thickening of frontal

[Supraorbital area missing]

Lateral profile shows gentle curvature of frontal plane; then slopes steeply from bregma to lambda

Cranial capacity 880 ml

Small area for insertion of neck muscles is small; may be pathological (Hublin, 1985)

Mastoid process

External auditory meatus

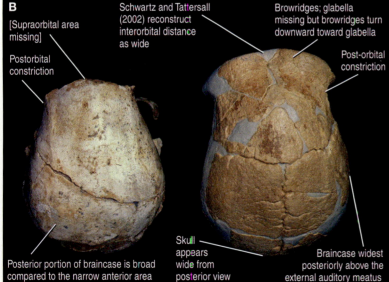

B

[Supraorbital area missing]

Postorbital constriction

Schwartz and Tattersall (2002) reconstruct interorbital distance as wide

Browridges; glabella missing but browridges turn downward toward glabella

Post-orbital constriction

Posterior portion of braincase is broad compared to the narrow anterior area

Skull appears wide from posterior view

Braincase widest posteriorly above the external auditory meatus

3.103 A Right lateral comparison of Saldanha (top; "early archaic" *H. sapiens*) and Sale (bottom; *H. erectus* or "early archaic" *H. sapiens*). **B** Dorsal contrast of Sale (left) and Saldanha (right). The Saldanha skull is from Elandsfontein, South Africa and is dated to about 500,000 yrs (BP). Sale is from El Hamra, Morocco and is dated to the Middle Pleistocene (200,000–500,000 yrs BP. Holloway (1981, 2000) estimates the Sale cranial capacity at 880 ml, while Saldanha has a cranial capacity of 1,225 ml. Rightmire (1990) has discussed the Sale braincase. It is small (perhaps female) and thick-walled, with appreciable postorbital constriction, blunt keeling along the midline of the narrow frontal squama, large mastoid processes (for a small skull), rounded occipital bone, but without a postglenoid process (unlike Sangiran 2, which has a small postglenoid process). The greatest breadth of the skull is at the level of the supramastoid crests. While Rightmire (1990:) states that, "The characters of the skull do not point unequivocally toward an identification as *H. erectus,*" he enumerates features typical of *H. erectus*: frontal form, shape of temporal squama, overall proportions of the braincase, thick vault bones and an endocranial capacity below the mean for *H. erectus*. There are some more modern features, such as a short basioccipital and some other features that may be pathological, but he places the skull within *H. erectus*.

Photos by C. Tarka, courtesy and copyright © Laboratoire d'Anthropologie, Universite de Bordeaux I (Talence), South African Museum (Cape Town) and Dr. Eric Delson

Morphological Features of "Early Archaic H. sapiens"

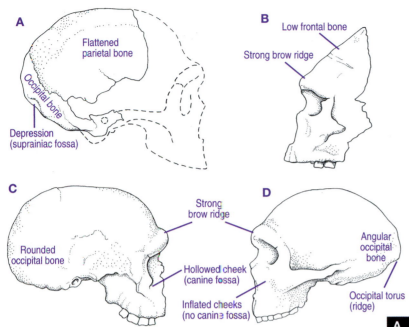

3.104 Comparison of four European middle Pleistocene fossil hominid skulls from Stringer and Gamble (1993:67), depicting characteristic features and contrasting dissimilarities. **A** Swanscome. **B** Arago 21. **C** Steinheim. **D** Petralona.

In Search of the Neanderthals by C. Stringer and Gamble, copyright © 1993. Reprinted by permission of Thames and Hudson

Omo

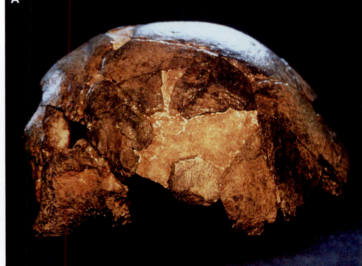

3.105 Left lateral aspect of the Omo Kibish 2 skull from the Kibish Formation, Omo, Ethiopia, upper Pleistocene (about 130,000 yrs BP).

Courtesy of Dr. Osbjorn Pearson. Specimen courtesy of Institute of Human Origins and National Museum of Ethiopia

3.106 Omo Kibish 1 skull from the Kibish Formation, Omo, Ethiopia. **A** Right lateral view. **B** Posterior view. It is estimated to be the same age of Omo 2.

Courtesy of Dr. Osbjorn Pearson. Specimen courtesy of Institute of Human Origins and National Museum of Ethiopia

Kabwe 1

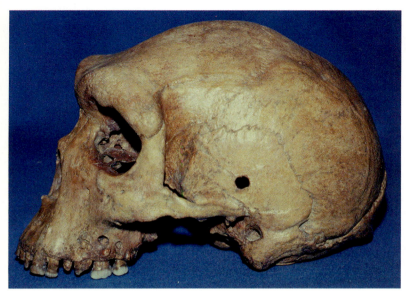

3.107 Left lateral aspect of the Kabwe 1 skull, also called Broken Hill or "Rhodesian Man" from Broken Hill Mine, Zambia. It is probable that the skull is older than 125,000 years, but its precise date is uncertain (Schwartz and Tattersall, 2002). It is an almost complete skull, missing its lower right side and an appreciable amount of the basicranium. Several teeth are missing; those that are present show heavy wear to the crowns. The specimen has generally been referred to early archaic *H. sapiens*, following Brauer (1984) but also has been recently called *H. heidelbergensis* (Schwartz and Tattersall, 2002) or *H. rhodesiensis* (Woodward, 1921; McBrearty and Brooks, 2000). Rightmire (1990:212) states that the cranium is low in outline and has heavy browridges: "The supraorbital torus is thicker than that of most other Pleistocene hominids [hominins] and is even heavier than that of OH 9." The face is large and is particularly broad across the orbits. The frontal bone is flattened on either side of a midline keel. There is significant postorbital constriction. Maximum cranial breadth is in the supramastoid area, as in *H. erectus*.

Courtesy of Dr. G. Philip Rightmire

Ndutu

3.108 Left lateral aspect of the Ndutu skull from the area around Lake Ndutu, Tanzania, discovered by A. Mturi in 1973. There have been various dates proposed for the specimen, from about 200,000 (Schwartz and Tattersall, 2002) to 400,000 years (Leakey and Hay, 1982). The specimen is missing portions of the right side of the face, most of the maxillae, basicranium and portions of the cranial vault. There are, therefore, sections in the specimen that have been reconstructed. It has been placed in both *H. erectus* and archaic *H. sapiens* by various workers, and recently has been said to have "affinities with *Homo heidelbergensis*" (Schwartz and Tattersall, 2002: 188). Rightmire (1990) estimates a range of 1,070–1,120 ml for cranial capacity, with an average of 1,100 ml. There is no evidence of a suprainiac crest (unlike Neanderthals), and the anatomy of the supratoral sulcus and the presence of an occipital protuberance differentiate it from *H. erectus*. There is a well-developed transverse torus on the occipital and postorbital constriction is significant.

Courtesy of Dr. G Philip Rightmire

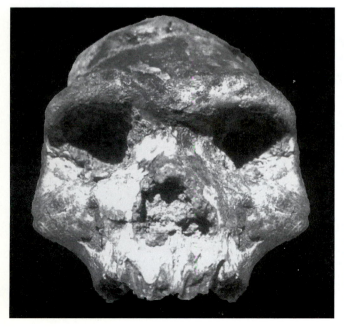

3.109 Frontal view of the Bodo D'Ar skull. The face of Bodo D'Ar was recovered in two major pieces by Asfaw and Whitehead. Additional fragments were mapped by Wood and Whitehead (Kalb *et al*, 1980) and collected by members of the Rift Valley Research Mission in Ethiopia. Details of the discovery are in Whitehead (1982) and Kalb (2001). The site is on the east side of the Awash River, 56 km SSW of the fossil site at Hadar. The photograph of the original specimen was by Mebrate. The specimen lacks the right side of the face below the orbit, so the right zygomatic region is reconstructed from the left side (Photoshop reconstruction by Kappelman). After an initial description (Conroy *et al*, 1978), Rightmire (1996) did a much more comprehensive study, in which he pointed-out that the braincase is low, "decidedly archaic in appearance," with thick skull bones. The frontal profile is flattened and the supraorbital torus is projecting. There is keeling of the midline and a bregmatic eminence that are like those of *H. erectus*. Postorbital constriction is moderate. Cranial capacity is 1,250 ml, which is greater than in *H. erectus*. Rightmire (1996) groups Bodo D'Ar with Broken Hill in *H. heidelbergensis*. White (1986) maintains that there are intentional cutmarks on the skull.

Courtesy of Mr. Jon Kalb.

Specimen courtesy of Institute of Human Origins and National Museum of Ethiopia

Tighenif and Mauer

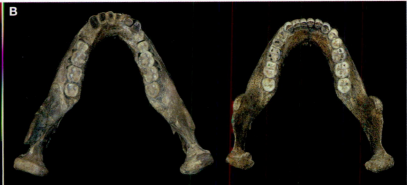

3.110 **A** Right lateral comparison of Tighenif 3 (upper) and Mauer I (GPIH) (lower) mandibles. **B** Occlusal views of same specimens with Tighenif 3 on left and Mauer I on right. Note that neither specimen has a chin. Tighenif 3 is the largest of the three mandibles from this locality and has been viewed as male because of its robusticity. It shows restricted retromolar spaces, a high and large coronoid process, symphyseal face that is flattened anteriorly, and "the entire ramus is large by modern standards" (Rightmire, 1990:129). The Mauer mandible was found near Heidelberg, Germany and is believed to be about 500,000 years old (Schwartz and Tattersall, 2002). It is the holotype of *H. heidelbergensis* (Schoetensack, 1908). It often has been included in that group of specimens considered to be "archaic" *H. sapiens*, which various workers are now assigning to *H. heidelbergensis*. It is characterized by a very robust, thick mandibular body. The condylar process is present but the coronoid process is broken and therefore the ramus has a shorter appearance than would have been the case in life.   Courtesy of and copyright © Dr. Eric Delson

Arago and Steinheim

3.111 **A** Right lateral views of Steinheim (top) and Arago 21 (bottom). **B** Frontal comparison of Steinheim (left) and Arago 21 (right). Steinheim is from near Stuttgart, Germany and may be 225,000 years old (Schwartz and Tattersall, 2002). It has an estimated cranial capacity of 1,100 cc. The Arago 21 fossil is from the area near Tautavel, France and may be about 450,000 years old (Schwartz and Tattersall, 2002). Stringer and Gamble (1994) describe the Steinheim skull as possessing a low, narrow forehead with a strong browridge, and the back of the skull appears to have a suprainiac fossa. Arago 21 has strong brow ridges, a narrow frontal area and a brain size of about 1,200 ml. It has a flat face, low broad nose and low orbits, which Stringer and Gamble (1994) view as suggesting a larger version of Steinheim.

Photos by C. Tarka, courtesy and copyright © Institut de Paléontologie Humaine (Paris), Staatliches Museum fur Naturkunde (Stuttgart), and Dr. Eric Delson

Petralona

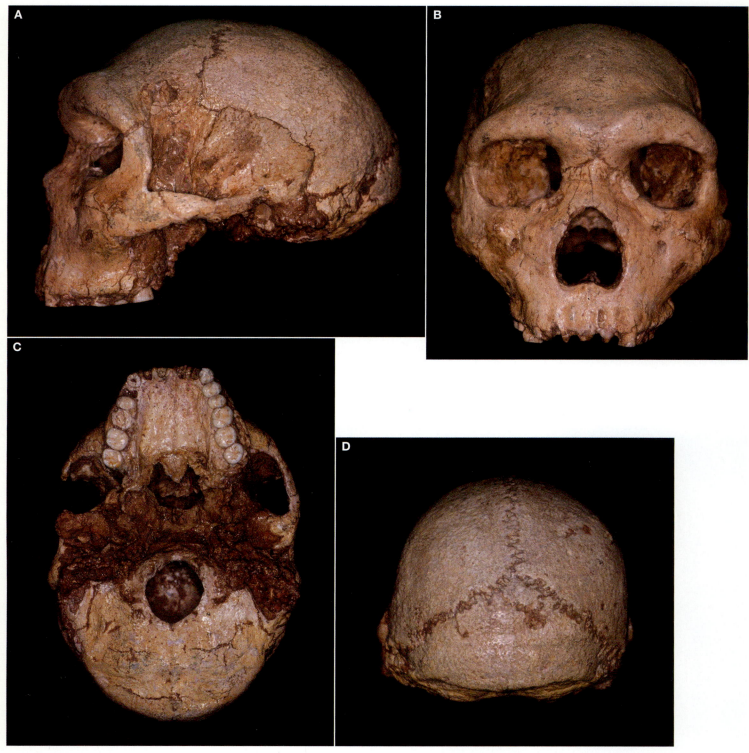

3.112 Petralona cranium. **A** Left lateral aspect. **B** Frontal aspect. **C** Basicranial aspect. **D** Posterior aspect. In posterior view, the sagittal and lambdoid sutures are apparent, as is lambda. The specimen has received considerable study (e.g., Murrill, 1981; Rightmire, 1990; Stringer *et al*, 1979) and has been variously called a Neanderthal (Mann and Trinkaus, 1973), *Homo erectus* (Hemmer, 1972) or *Homo heidelbergensis* (Stringer and Gamble, 1994). Schwartz and Tattersall (2002) quote a cranial capacity of 1,220 ml. Dating of the cave site has been controversial; it is perhaps between 150,000-250,000 years old. Rightmire (1990) states that the frontal bone is flattened, there is minimal supratoral sulcus, the supraorbital torus is heavy and it is divided into separate arches. There is less postorbital constriction than in Broken Hill, and there is no keeling along the midline—in these ways, it is more similar to Arago 21. The face is large and the biorbital breadth is similar to Broken Hill. The midface is heavily built.

Courtesy of and copyright © Dr. Eric Delson

Narmada

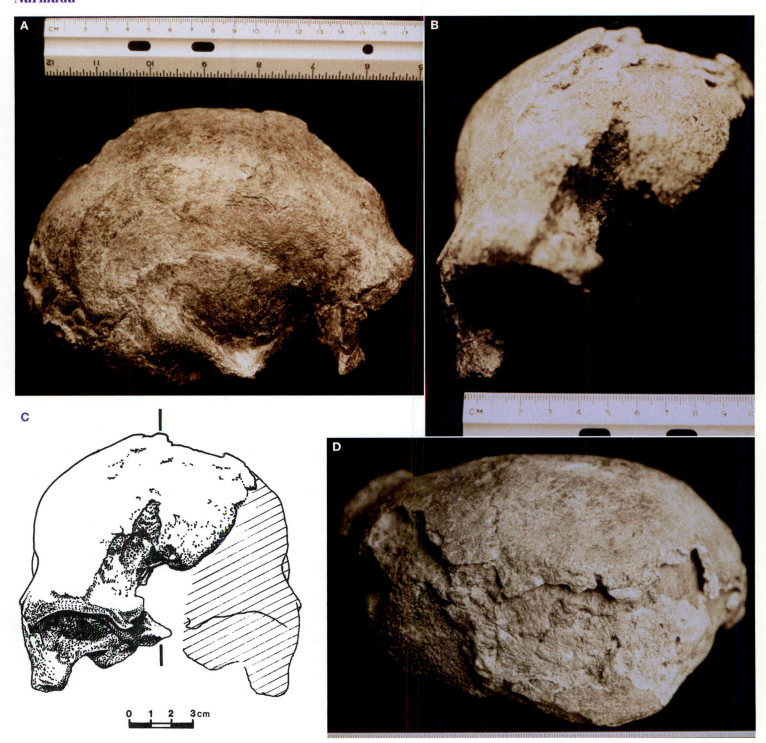

3.113 Narmada skull. **A** Right lateral view. **B** Frontal view. **C** Frontal reconstruction view. **D** Superior view. The specimen was found by Sonakia on the bank of the Narmada River in Madhya Pradesh, India. Faunal dating suggests a late Middle Pleistocene or early Late Pleistocene date. Kennedy *et al* (1991) compared the features of the skull with those listed by Rightmire (1988) as typical of *H. erectus*. Narmada has a larger cranial capacity, a higher cranial vault, less flattening of the frontal bone, higher minimal frontal breadth, broader mandibular (condylar) fossa, and other features that distinguish it from *H. erectus*. They (p. 492) conclude that the specimen is *H. sapiens narmadensis* and it "exhibits a broad spectrum of morphological traits that occur in specimens from Petralona, Bilzingsleben, Kabwe, Dali, and Ngangdong, but are reflected, too, in possible Neanderthal antecedents of Steinheim, Swanscombe, Ehringsdorf, and Fontechevade."

Courtesy of Dr. K.A.R. Kennedy, Cornell University and the University of Allahabad, India

Dali

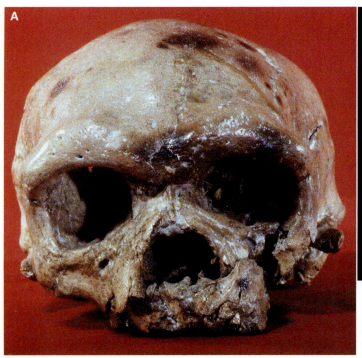

3.114 Dali cranium. **A** Frontal aspect. **B** Left lateral aspect. The specimen was discovered in 1978 by Shuntang Liu near Jiefang Village, Dali County, Shaanxi Province, China. Wu and Poirier (1995) describe the skull as fairly complete and robust. The supraorbital torus is thick. They view it as being more similar to archaic *H. sapiens* than to *H. erec-tus* in that the broadest portion of the skull vault is near the temporal squama rather than near the cranial base (unlike the Zhoukoutian material). The upper portion of the parietal is more horizontal, and the lower part more vertical, than in *H. erectus*. The postorbital constriction is broader than in *H. erectus*. Metric data indicates that the skull is intermediate between *H. erectus* and modern *H. sapiens*, and within the range of archaic *H. sapiens*. At the same time, there are thick skull bones, prominent brow ridges, and a low position of the zygomatic arch—features that are similar to those of *H. erectus*. The cranial capacity is 1,120 ml (Holloway, 2000). Dali is dated to the late Middle Pleistocene, perhaps 230,000–180,000 years BP.

Photo A courtesy of Dr. Xinzhi Wu; Photo B courtesy of and copyright © Dr. Eric Delson

Neandertals: *Homo sapiens neanderthalensis* or *Homo neanderthalensis*?

The characters of Neandertals can be divided into those that are primitive, those that they appear to share with anatomically modern humans, and their own unique characters that are found mainly within the Neandertals (Stringer, 1988). Primitive features include: a long, low braincase (which we saw in *H. erectus*) which is flattened on the superior surface, a short parietal arch, a well-developed supraorbital torus that is particularly strong near the midline, large face, large nasal aperture, a large dentition (especially the incisors), a broad basicranium that is usually flatter than that found in anatomically modern humans, and a mandible that generally does not have a chin. Characters that Neandertals share with anatomically modern humans consist of: lateral reduction of the brow-ridge, reduction of the occipital torus (in contrast to *H. erectus*), relatively rounder occipital profile, longer occipital plane, large

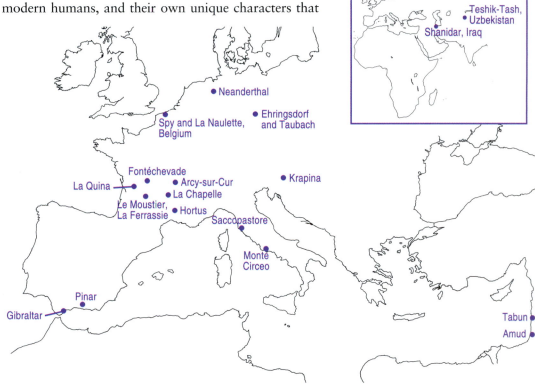

3.115 Map of major discovery sites of Neandertal fossil material.

brain (sometimes larger than that found in modern humans), and reduced facial prognathism (compared to *H. erectus*). The unique features include: spherical shape of the cranial vault in posterior aspect, posterior position of the maximum breadth of the skull, possession of a suprainiac fossa, prominent juxtamastoid crest, large nose, "swept-back" and inflated cheekbones (similar to Bodo D'Ar), possession of a retromolar space behind

the third molars, and a unique shape to the mandibular foramen. Interestingly, their average cranial capacity is greater than that found in modern humans, but their brains were low, broadest at the base, with small frontal lobes and large occipital lobes (see Table 2.6).

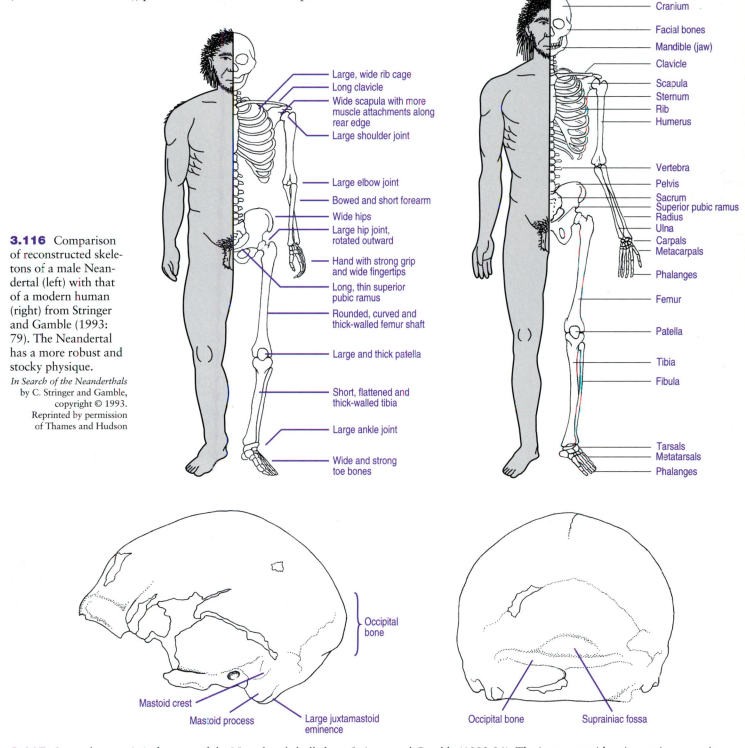

3.116 Comparison of reconstructed skeletons of a male Neandertal (left) with that of a modern human (right) from Stringer and Gamble (1993: 79). The Neandertal has a more robust and stocky physique.

In Search of the Neanderthals by C. Stringer and Gamble, copyright © 1993. Reprinted by permission of Thames and Hudson

Large, wide rib cage
Long clavicle
Wide scapula with more muscle attachments along rear edge
Large shoulder joint

Large elbow joint
Bowed and short forearm
Wide hips
Large hip joint, rotated outward
Hand with strong grip and wide fingertips
Long, thin superior pubic ramus
Rounded, curved and thick-walled femur shaft

Large and thick patella

Short, flattened and thick-walled tibia

Large ankle joint

Wide and strong toe bones

Cranium
Facial bones
Mandible (jaw)
Clavicle
Scapula
Sternum
Rib
Humerus

Vertebra
Pelvis
Sacrum
Superior pubic ramus
Radius
Ulna
Carpals
Metacarpals
Phalanges

Femur

Patella

Tibia
Fibula

Tarsals
Metatarsals
Phalanges

Occipital bone

Mastoid crest
Mastoid process
Large juxtamastoid eminence

Occipital bone   Suprainiac fossa

3.117 Some characteristic features of the Neandertal skull, from Stringer and Gamble (1993:84). The juxtamastoid eminence is a conspicuous crest found at the inferior edge of the occipital, posterior to and generally larger than the mastoid process. The mastoid is more prominent in modern humans. The suprainiac fossa is a pit in the middle of the occipital in Neandertals, produced by the neck muscles. Modern humans, in contrast, tend to have an occipital protuberance in the area.

In Search of the Neanderthals by C. Stringer and Gamble, copyright © 1993. Reprinted by permission of Thames and Hudson

Neandertal and Krapina

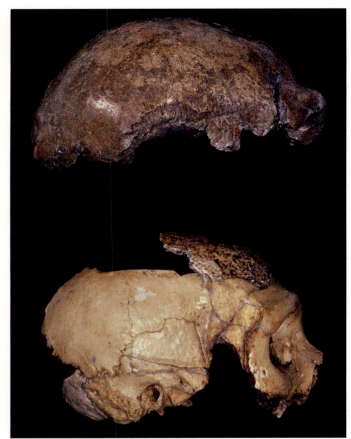

3.118 Right lateral aspects of the Neandertal (upper) and Krapina C (lower) fossils. The Neandertal fossil is from Hochdahl, Germany and is dated to the upper Pleistocene (35,000–70,000 yrs BP). Krapina C is from Croatia and is dated to 130,000 yrs BP.

Photos by C. Tarka, courtesy and copyright © Geolosko-Paleontolosko Musej (Zagreb), Rheinisches Landesmuseum (Bonn), and Dr. Eric Delson

Neanderthal and La Ferrassie 1

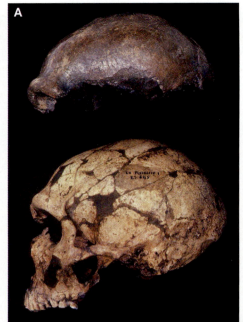

3.119 A Left lateral views of Neandertal (above) and La Ferrassie 1 (bottom). **B** Superior views of Neandertal (left) and La Ferrassie 1 (right). The latter fossil is from Savignac du Bugue, Dordogne, France and is dated to 40,000-50,000 yrs. BP.

Photos by C. Tarka, courtesy and copyright © Musée de l'Homme (Paris), Rheinisches Landesmuseum (Bonn), and Dr. Eric Delson

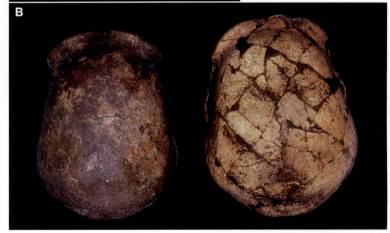

La Ferrassie 1, Saccopastore 1, and Krapina C

3.120 A Frontal view of La Ferrassie 1 (left) and Saccopastore 1 (right). **B** Right lateral view of Krapina C (top) and Saccopastore 1 (bottom). The latter fossil is from Rome, Italy, and is dated to about 120,000–130,00 years BP. It is a Neandertal, but has a small

brain (1,250 cc; Holloway, 2000). La Ferrassie 1 is judged to be a male, "classic" western European Neandertal; it may be younger than 70,000 years old (Schwartz and Tattersall, 2002). It's cranial capacity is believed to be about 1,640 cc (Holloway, 1985). Krapina C is perhaps 130,000 years old and is an adult Neandertal. It is perhaps more modern-looking than some other specimens because of its gracile supraorbital tori and lack of a supratoral sulcus.

Photos by C. Tarka, courtesy and copyright © Museo di Antropologia "G. Sergi" (Dipartimento di Biologia Animale e dell'Uomo, Universitá di Roma "La Sapienza"), Geolosko-Paleontolosko Musej (Zagreb), Musée de l'Homme (Paris), and Dr. Eric Delson

La Quina 5 and St. Cesaire

3.121 Right lateral view of La Quina 5 (top), without maxilla and mandible, and St. Cesaire (bottom). La Quina is a "classic" from Charente, Gardes-le-Pontaroux, France and is dated to 40,000–55,000 yrs. BP. Holloway (1985) estimates its cranial capacity to be 1,350 cc. St. Cesaire is a Neandertal from western France. It was discovered with Chatelperronian tools rather than the Mousterian type usually associated with Neandertals, although it is usually considered to be "classic" Neandertal in terms of its morphology, and it is an example of a deliberate burial. The date of the Saint Cesaire material is probably about 36,500 +/- 2,700 years; it, therefore, demonstrates that later Neandertals were contemporaneous with anatomically modern humans.

Photos by C. Tarka, courtesy and copyright © Laboratoire de'Anthropologie, Université de Bordeaux I (Talence), Musée de l'Homme (Paris), and Dr. Eric Delson

Pech de l'Aze

3.123 Pech de l'Aze Neandertal child skull dated between 45,000–55,000 yrs BP. **A** Right lateral view. **B** Frontal view. Schwartz and Tattersall (2002) estimate that it was 4 years old at the time of its death and had a cranial capacity of 1,150 cc. It was discovered in a cave in the Dordogne of France in 1909. As a child, its morphology is somewhat different from that expected in an adult Neandertal, with a long but broad skull, no supraorbital tori, ovoid orbits, and metopic suture still present.

La Ferrassie 1 and Amud 1

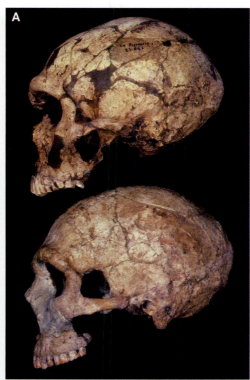

3.122 A Left lateral views of La Ferrassie 1 (top) and Amud 1 (bottom). **B** Frontal views of Amud 1 (left) and La Ferrassie 1 (right). Amud 1 is from Wadi Amud, Israel, and is dated to 35,000–45,000 yrs. BP.

Photos by C. Tarka, courtesy and copyright © Israel Antiquities Authority (Jerusalem), Musée de l'Homme (Paris), and Dr. Eric Delson

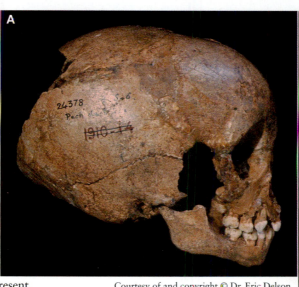

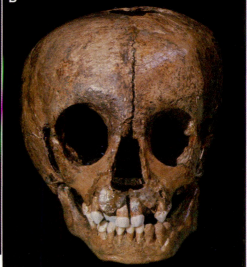

Courtesy of and copyright © Dr. Eric Delson

Shanidar

Shanidar is a cave site in the Zagros Mountains of Iraq. It was excavated by Ralph Solecki and associates in three field seasons during 1953–1960 (Solecki, 1971). The site has yielded the largest number of Neanderthal fossils from the Middle East—nine individuals, some of which may have been deliberately buried (Stringer and Gamble, 1994). The two specimens that are figured here are from Layer D, estimated to be 60,000 years old (Schwartz and Tattersall, 2002). Both of the skulls below are from adult skeletons.

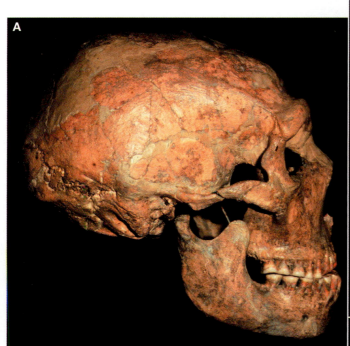

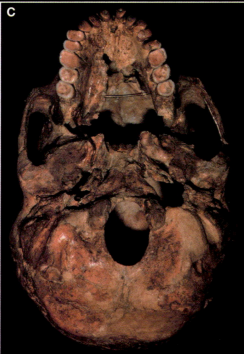

3.124 Shanidar 1. **A** Right lateral view. **B** Frontal view. **C** Basicranial view. **D** Superior view. Trinkaus (1983:56) views the reconstruction, which had been accomplished by Dr. T. D. Stewart, as "undoubtedly close to the original shape" and describes the specimen. He considers many of its features to be characteristic of Neandertals (note in lateral view): long, low and relatively narrow cranial vault; large, rounded supraorbital torus; moderate supratoral sulcus; prognathic midface; elongated mandible without a chin; curvature of the occipital bone; form of the transverse occipital torus; development of the occipitomastoid crests; and shape and size of mastoid processes. In contrast to other Neandertals and to modern humans, the frontal profile is flatter and the parietal arc is more curved. It is distinct from other Neandertals in the slight development of the occipital bun, large size and development of the suprainiac fossa, and coalescence of the anterior mastoid tubercles with the mastoid crests. The right orbit (frontal view) is not as classically round as is typically described for Neandertals, especially the European representatives, and its maxillae are "minimally inflated." Its large orbits probably caused it to have a narrow interorbital breadth, below Amud 1, Tabun C1 and at the lower range of the European fossils. The nasal aperture is small but its nasal cavity is large. The specimen manifests a traumatic crushing fracture to the left lateral orbit and zygomatic bone, which significantly affects facial morphology (Trinkaus, pers. comm.).

By permission of Dr. Erik Trinkaus

3.125 Frontal view of the anterior dentition and jaws of Shanidar 1. The mandible is large but does not have a prominent chin. It does have a well-developed symphyseal tuberosity and lateral tubercles. The body of the mandible is elongated, although it manifests typical Neandertal morphology (Trinkaus, 1983). Note the heavy occlusal wear on the anterior teeth. Trinkaus (1983) reports that most of the anterior teeth have lost their crowns. By permission of Dr. Erik Trinkaus

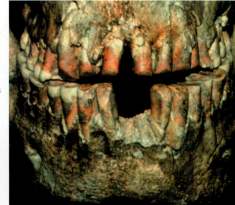

3.126 Shanidar 5. **A** Left lateral view. **B** Frontal view. The specimen was cleaned and assembled by Dr. Erik Trinkaus in 1976. He (1983) describes the specimen, identifies three areas that may show some distortion, and states that it is the second most complete Shanidar cranium. The fossil has a heavily built and long cranial vault, low frontal arch, high parietal arc, high position of lambda, rugose mastoid process, an external auditory meatus with an anteroinferior-posterosuperior orientation and in-line with the long axis of the zygomatic process. Trinkaus (1983:134), following Vallois (1969), recognizes the latter as "a typically Neandertal characteristic that distinguishes them from recent humans." The face of the specimen is among the largest in Neandertals and falls within the Neandertal range of variation in projection from the neurocranium. It has a thin supraorbital torus which is thickest near the medial side of the orbit; in this, it is similar to Shanidar 1, different from Shanidar 4, but not as extreme as some European Late Neandertals. The supratoral sulcus is shallow near the midline. Trinkaus (1983:138) states that the orbits "follow the general Neandertal pattern of being quite rounded, especially along their superior margins." Its interorbital breadth is near the middle of the European Neandertal range of variation, but is biorbital breadth is relatively large. It has a very large nasal region. Shanidar 5 has inflated maxillae and "considerable" midfacial prognathism, although less than Shanidar 1.

By permission of Dr. Erik Trinkaus

Skhul IV

3.127 The specimen is from Skhul Cave, Mount Carmel, Israel, and is dated to 80,000–100,000 yrs BP. It is considered to be a "Levantine Neandertal." Its browridges are less developed than those in Skhul V.

Courtesy of Dr. Osbjorn Pearson

ANATOMICALLY MODERN *HOMO SAPIENS*

3.128 Map of some major fossil sites of modern *Homo sapiens*.

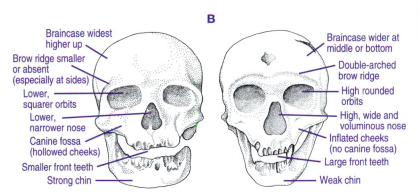

Comparison of the Skull of the Neandertal with that of the Anatomically Modern Human

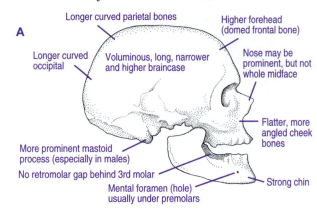

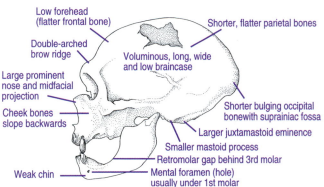

3.129 A Comparison of the cranial morphology of a modern *Homo sapiens* (Cro-Magnon 1, top) with a Neandertal (La Chapelle-aux-Saints, bottom). **B** Frontal comparison (Cro-Magnon 1, left), (La Chapelle-aux-Saints, right).

In Search of the Neanderthals by C. Stringer and Gamble, copyright © 1993. Reprinted by permission of Thames and Hudson

3.130 A Right lateral view of the Neandertal Amud 1 (top) and the modern *H. sapiens* Skhul 5 (bottom). **B** Frontal views. Amud 1 is from a cave in Wadi Amud, Israel and was discovered in 1961 by H. Suzuki and collaborators. It is a fairly complete specimen, although in poor condition, missing a large portion of the basicranium and found at the top of a Middle Paleolithic archeological level. The age of the specimen is in the 42–49 Ka range. Skhul 5 is from Wadi el-Mughara, Israel; there are differing dates for the specimen, varying from 31,000–33,000 yrs BP to 80,000–120,000yrs BP. The individual was intentionally buried in a flexed position and clutching the jaw of a wild boar. Amud 1 is the tallest Neandertal discovered to date, reconstructed at 5'10" and has the largest brain capacity of any known hominin. It is considered to be male despite its thin browridges, and it has a more developed chin than do the Shanidar Neandertals (Stringer and Gamble, 1994). Amud is, however, similar to Tabun and Shanidar in possessing a long, broad and low skull, double-arched browridge, a large face with a large nose, midfacial prognathism, large palate and lower jaw with less chin development than in modern *H. sapiens*. In contrast, Skhul V is more modern in its appearance and is similar to Qafzeh, with high and short crania "rounded in profile but, unlike Neandertals, parallel-sided rather than spherical in posterior view" (Stringer and Gamble, 1994:101). The specimen has a well-developed browridge, but its shape is different from that of the Neandertals. There is a broad but low nasal opening. Midfacial projection is not developed. The cheekbones are "hollowed" rather than flat or inflated and are not "swept-back." The orbits are wide and low. The upper face is broad. The lower face is projecting. Forehead development is appreciable. The mandible is shorter than in the Neandertal without forward positioning of the teeth that produces the retromolar space. See Wolpoff (1980:346) for a general comparison of the morphological features in the earliest anatomically modern *H. sapiens* with Neandertals.

Photos by C. Tarka, courtesy and copyright © Israel Antiquities Authority (Jerusalem), Musée de l'Homme (Paris), and Dr. Eric Delson

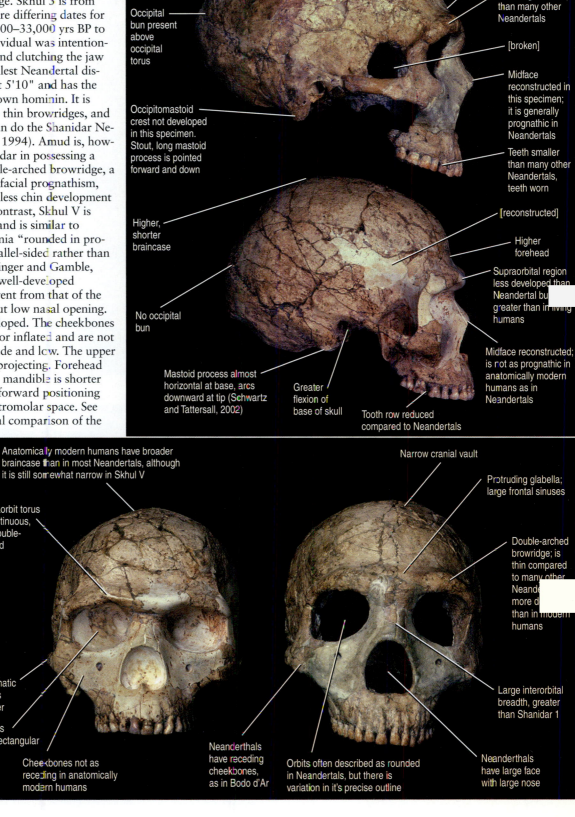

A

Neandertal cranium rounded especially in posterior view

Long, low skull but Amud 1 has large brain (1,740 ml)

Receding forehead

Supratoral sulcus

Browridge smaller than many other Neandertals

Occipital bun present above occipital torus

[broken]

Midface reconstructed in this specimen; it is generally prognathic in Neandertals

Occipitomastoid crest not developed in this specimen. Stout, long mastoid process is pointed forward and down

Teeth smaller than many other Neandertals, teeth worn

[reconstructed]

Higher, shorter braincase

Higher forehead

Supraorbital region less developed than Neandertal but greater than in living humans

No occipital bun

Midface reconstructed; is not as prognathic in anatomically modern humans as in Neandertals

Mastoid process almost horizontal at base, arcs downward at tip (Schwartz and Tattersall, 2002)

Greater flexion of base of skull

Tooth row reduced compared to Neandertals

B

Anatomically modern humans have broader braincase than in most Neandertals, although it is still somewhat narrow in Skhul V

Narrow cranial vault

Protruding glabella; large frontal sinuses

Supraorbit torus is continuous, not double-arched

Double-arched browridge; is thin compared to many other Neande... more d... than in modern humans

Zygomatic arch is slender

Orbits subrectangular

Large interorbital breadth, greater than Shanidar 1

Cheekbones not as receding in anatomically modern humans

Neanderthals have receding cheekbones, as in Bodo d'Ar

Orbits often described as rounded in Neandertals, but there is variation in it's precise outline

Neanderthals have large face with large nose

Paleolithic *Homo sapiens*

Skhul V

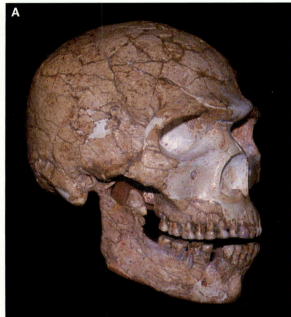

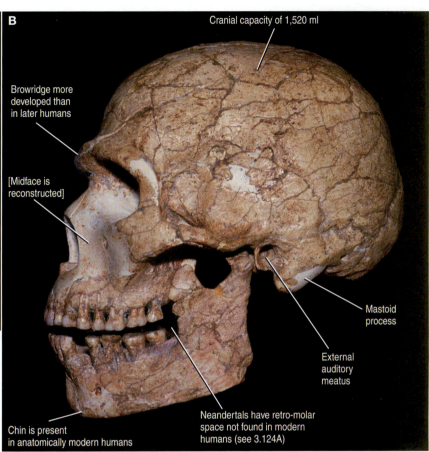

Cranial capacity of 1,520 ml

Browridge more developed than in later humans

[Midface is reconstructed]

Mastoid process

External auditory meatus

Chin is present in anatomically modern humans

Neandertals have retro-molar space not found in modern humans (see 3.124A)

3.131 Skhul 5. **A** Right oblique view. **B** Left lateral view.   Courtesy of and copyright © Dr. Eric Delson

Cro-Magnon 2

3.132 Left lateral aspect of the adult female Cro-Magnon 2 partial skull. The specimen is from Les Eyzies, Dordogne, France and is considered to be fully modern *H. sapiens* from the Würm glaciation, between 23,000–27,000 yrs BP. Cro-Magnum 2 is smaller and more gracile than are the two males (Cro-Magnon 1, 3) and is partially distorted. Sexual dimorphism appears to be greater in the Cro-Magnon cranial vault than in the face, as the face of Cro-Magnon 2 is about the same size as in Cro-Magnon 1 (Wolpoff, 1980). The anatomically modern nature of the skull is illustrated by it "domed" nature, well-developed frontal and parietal eminences, vertical sides, rounded posterior aspect, thin supraorbital margins, subsquare orbits, and thin bones of the cranial vault. The skull is, however, long and the palate is somewhat long. This is consistent with Wolpoff's (1980:346) generalization that, "The early modern *Homo sapiens* crania are, on the average, taller and narrower than but the same length as Neandertal crania of the same sex."

Courtesy of and copyright © Dr. Eric Delson

Mladec 1 and 2

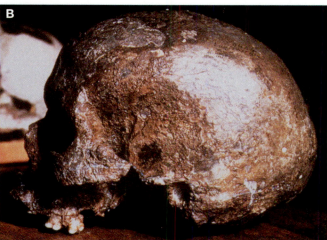

3.133 Mladec 1 skull, generally considered to be fully modern *H. sapiens* although Wolpoff (1980) underscores similarities to Neandertals in some specimens: he (p. 311) refers to Mldec as the "Skhul of Europe." **A** Superofrontal aspect. **B** Left lateral aspect. The specimen dates from Wurm II, therefore earlier than ca. 32,000 yrs BP. The superofrontal view emphasizes the facial, supraorbital, and forehead regions: contrast these to the photographs of the Neandertals.

Courtesy of Dr. Osbjorn Pearson

3.134 **A** Left oblique view of the Mladec 1 skull and palate #5487 (Wolpoff #8). **B** Comparison of Mladec 2 on left and Mladec 1 on right. Wolpoff (1988) states that both specimens are female. Mladec 1 has a "moderately developed" supraorbital torus, small mastoid processes and "marked posterior cranial flattening." In Contrast, Mladec 2 has no supraorbital torus, large mastoid processes and a higher, rounder back of the skull.

Courtesy of Austrian Museum

Dolni Vestonice 3

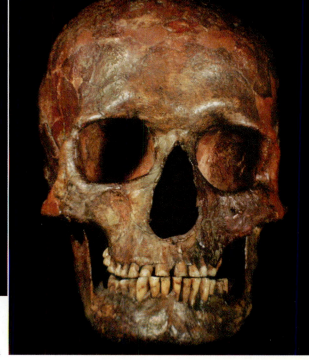

3.135 Dolni Vestonice 3 skull, considered to be fully modern *H. sapiens* from about 27,640 yrs BP. **A** Right lateral view. **B** Frontal view. Dolni Vestonice has open site burials in contrast to the Neandertal burials in Europe.

Courtesy of and copyright © Dr. Eric Delson

Pavlov 1

3.136 Left lateral close-up of the articulated maxilla and mandible of Pavlov 1, dated to about 26,000 yrs BP. Note the well-developed chin on the specimen and that the occlusal surfaces of most of the teeth (with the exception of the third lower molar) are worn flat.

Courtesy of and copyright © Dr. Eric Delson

Grotte des Enfants, Italian Riveria

3.137 Frontal view of the entire Grotte des Enfants 4 skeleton. The individual is described as a male Cro-Magnon from about 25,000 yrs. BP. The Grotte des Enfants adult crania are smaller and less robust than are the skull from Mladec (Wolpoff, 1980), rounded and with reduced development of the supraorbital area.

Courtesy of Prehistoric Anthropology in Monaco

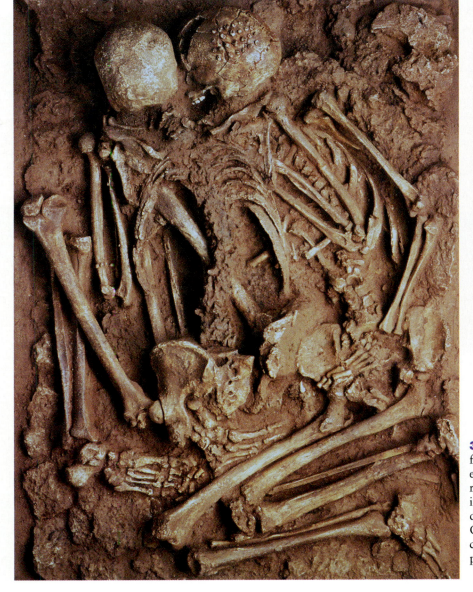

3.138 Grotte des Enfants 5 (adult female) and 6 (juvenile male) in discovered positions. The adult female has a reduced cranial breadth, is less robust in her facial skeleton and browridge development than in specimens such as Combe Capelle; she has small, angled cheekbones and her skull is short compared to its width (Wolpoff, 1980).

Courtesy of Prehistoric Anthropology in Monaco

Barma Grande

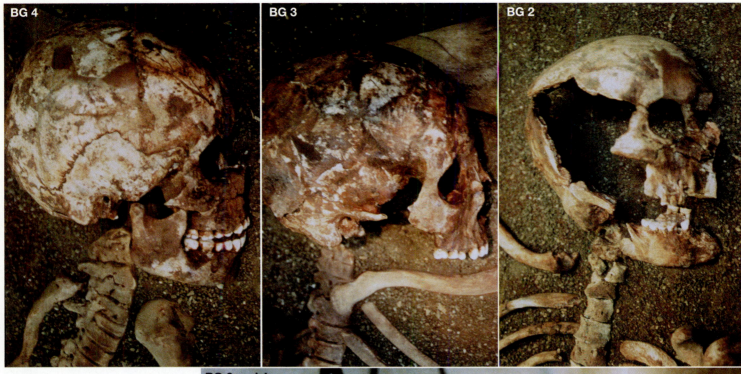

BG 4   BG 3   BG 2

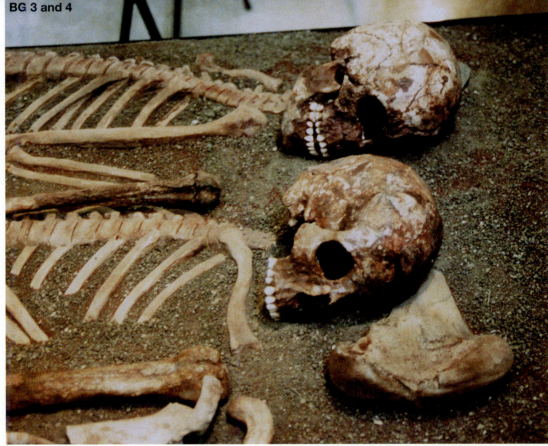

BG 3 and 4

3.139 Barma Grande 2-4 consist of a triple burial of Aurignacian archeological context, presumably at least 25,000 years old. The specimens are on exhibit at the Museo Preistorico dei Balzi Rossi, Ventimiglia, Italy. Verneau (1908) presents a summary of the discovery of the material, of their features and archeological context. Barma Grande is one of the caves in the complex near the village of Grimaldi in Italy. The first human skeleton was discovered by M. Louis Julien in February, 1884. M. Abbo found another human skeleton in February, 1892, as the cave was being dug out for agricultural purposes and the attention of archeologists was soon attracted to the site. Verneau (1908) reports that the skeletons were lying parallel to each other and were covered by red ochre. Verneau's (1908: 83) figure indicates that all three skeletons had mandibles although the middle specimen is without it in the display figured here. The specimen nearest the cave entrance (Barma Grande 2) was lying flat on its back and its skull was resting on its left side. The middle skeleton (Barma Grande 3) had its head propped against an ox femur (see figure here). The head of the third skeleton (Barma Grande 4) had its head resting on a flint knife. Associated with the three individuals were ornaments made of materials such as the canine teeth of deer, fish vertebrae and shells. Verneau (1906) provides an account of the skeletons from the Grotte du Cavillon, Barma Grande, Baousso da Torre and the Grotte des Enfants. Cartailhac (1912) is a detailed description of the archeology of the Grimaldi caves. Formicola (1998) is a more recent analysis of the Barma Grande skeletal material.

Courtesy of Dr. Osbjorn Pearson and special appreciation to the Museo Preistorico dei Balzi Rossi.
Su concessione del Ministero per i Beni e le Attività Culturali-Soprintendenza per i Beni Archeologici della Liguria

POST-PALEOLITHIC ANATOMICALLY MODERN HUMANS

India

The Mahadaha and Sarai Nahar Rai burials are associated with a stone tool tradition termed "microlithic." The tools were diminutive in size and the period also saw the introduction of the bow-and-arrow and composite harpoon-like tools. There is evidence of trade networks and cave paintings are found from the period. Sarai Nahar Rai is dated to the second millenium and Mahadaha to the third millenium. Kennedy (1999) describes the skeletons as robust and relatively taller than modern South Asians. They had large cheekteeth. Indications of trauma on bone are consistent with a hunting-gathering lifestyle, but there is little indication of the effect of infectious diseases on the bones or teeth.

3.140 The Mahadaha site was a cemetery with over 16 burials.

Courtesy of Dr. K.A.R. Kennedy, Cornell University and the University of Allahabad, India

3.141 A double burial (SNR 73-33) from Sarai Nahar Rai, Uttar Pradesh, India was found in proximity to a single burial (SNR 73-33/12). Interestingly, there is no evidence of caries in the teeth (Kennedy, 1999).

Courtesy of Dr. K.A.R. Kennedy, Cornell University and the University of Allahabad, India

Index

NOTES

NOTES

NOTES

NOTES